Preface

This study guide aims to:

- Explain the A1 programme, the different tasks you must accomplish (World Literature; the orals; the commentary and the exam essay) and how they are assessed

- Answer frequently asked questions about each of these areas (for example: *How do I write a commentary?*)

- Identify – through an Examiner's perspective – typical problem areas in each of the assessed components of A1, and provide some specific strategies for addressing these

- Suggest – from a teacher's perspective - guidelines and strategies for efficient learning and the development of necessary skills

- Provide samples of student work in each assessed area, to give you an idea of standards, and models to follow (all of a high 6 or 7 standard)

- Suggest some resources that can help you develop your work beyond the scope of this guide

It does not:

- Teach specific texts, though it does refer to some well-known texts when illustrating ideas

- Replace the teacher (nothing replaces a good teacher), though it aims to use some of the strategies and give some of the advice and guidance that a good teacher will provide

- Duplicate material that is published elsewhere. Suggestions for further reading and study are recommended and annotated in the bibliographies

It should be used:

- From the very beginning of the course, to accompany you through all the different aspects of the A1 programme and to help you build the essential skills you will need

- For revision in the final months of the programme, providing many suggestions to help you avoid typical pitfalls in the exam, and making a difference to your performance

****

Please send any comments or suggestions for future editions to Elizabeth Stephan (Language A1 Guide) c/o Oxford Study Courses: osc@osc-ib.com

Acknowledgements

This Guide could not have been written without the generous cooperation of a number of colleagues and students. Very grateful thanks to Richard Savage and Maureen Catt of St John's International School Belgium; to Tina Shobbrook, Jim Reese, Helen Martin and Tim Williams of the International School of Brussels; to Dr. Chris Greenhalge of Sevenoaks School, UK; Ms Anne Peters of Athens College, Greece; Andrew Flory of Skagerak International School Norway; and Andrew Howard of Hockerill Anglo-European College, UK, for their kind support and contributions.

Thanks are due also to students (most of them now alumni of their schools) who gave permission for their work to be included as samples: Eirini Spetza of Athens College; Anna Williams and Ananya Chakravarti of the International School of Brussels; Yazan Kopty, Antonia Strom, Joanna Rhodes, Laura Waggoner, Anna Arco, Laura Bell and Claire Anderson-Wheeler of St John's International School Belgium. My appreciation and thanks to the 'student readers' of Hockerill Anglo-European College, UK: Ricky Wyatt, Annabel Watts and Suzanne Battersby who read and commented on parts of the manuscript.

Special thanks to Tanya Stephan for her meticulous editing and formatting, and the gift of her time; to Andrew Harvey for his patient support and assistance throughout; and to colleague and Principal Examiner Elizabeth Druce, who read the drafts and on whose experience, judgement and cooperation I greatly depended.

Non-exclusive permission is granted to reprint "The Black Lace Fan My Mother Gave Me" by Eavan Boland, From *Outside History* (1990:Carcanet Press Limited)

Permission to reprint a passage from the opening of *The Horse's Mouth* by Joyce Cary (1944, Penguin) is kindly granted by the Joyce Carey Estate, c/o Andrew Lownie Associates, 17 Sutherland Street, London.

Permission is granted from The International Baccalaureate Organization, Cardiff, UK, to reprint the questions from May 1999, Paper One (Standard Level) on the Prose Commentary; and the following questions from Paper Two, May 2001 (Higher Level): *Drama:* Question 1 (b); *Prose: The Novel and the Short Story Question 3 (a)*.

For Joseph and Lizzie, with much love

Contents

Chapter Three: the Examination Essay

Chapter Four: Internal Assessment – the oral component   **65**

Introduction to the A1 Programme
and what you have to produce

It may be helpful at this point to see what an A1 programme looks like and to list the tasks you will need to accomplish. Four of the five chapters that follow then deal in detail with each assessed component, showing you what it is, and how you do it.

An A1 programme

Each school puts together its own programme of texts drawn from a list of authors supplied by the IB (Prescribed Book List). The following is a sample. Each school programme is different. Particular texts are not prescribed. Higher Level study 15 texts; Standard Level 11. Texts are not taught in the following order and may not be taught a Part at a time.

Part One (World Literature: H and S Level = 3 texts)
- *House of the Spirits*: Allende
- *Madame Bovary*: Flaubert
- *Chronicle of a Death Foretold*: Marquez

Outcome*:* World Literature Assignment One - 1,000-1,500-word comparative essay based on two texts. (See Chapter Five: World Literature)

Part Two (Texts for Detailed Study: H Level = 4 texts; S Level = 2 texts)
- *Hamlet*: Shakespeare
- Poems: Wilfred Owen; Robert Frost; Sylvia Plath
- Prose (Novel and Short Story): *The Scarlet Letter*: Hawthorne
- Prose (Non-fiction) *Chronicle of Youth: Great War Diary 1913-1917*: Vera Britten

Outcome: An individual, 15-minute oral commentary (See Chapter Four: Internal Assessment)

Part Three (Groups of Works, genre-based; H Level = 4 texts; S Level = 3 texts)
Choice of Genre – Drama (other genres may be novel, non-fiction, poetry)
- *A Streetcar Named Desire*: Williams
- *Equus*: Shaffer
- *The Crucible*: Miller
- *Medea*: Euripides (World Literature)

Outcome: A two-hour examination essay based on two or three of the works (See Chapter Three: The Examination Essay)

Part Four (Schools' Own Choice: H Level = 4 texts; S Level = 3 texts)
For this part the school may make its own choices of text including works outside the Book List
- *A Poetry Anthology*
- *Cat's Eye*: Atwood
- *Heart of Darkness*: Conrad
- *A Doll's House*: Ibsen (World Literature)

Outcome: An Individual 15-minute Oral Presentation based on one or more of the texts (See Chapter Four: Internal Assessment)

Further Outcomes:
1. A two-hour "unseen commentary" exam (See Chapter One: Commentary)
2. For Higher candidates only, a second World Literature Assignment, 1000-1500 words, based on any of the five World Literature texts not used in Assignment One (See Chapter Five)

Deadlines for the Northern Hemisphere:

The World Literature Assignments are sent away in late February of the second year.
The orals may be done (at the school) at any point up until March of the second year.
The two exams are set in May (or November) of the second year.

1. Introduction

The 'commentary' (Paper One of your exam), is worth 25% of your final grade, so it is worth considering ways of developing your skills in this during the course, as well as learning how to approach the exam successfully. Many students have never done a commentary before they enter the IB programme, and teachers vary considerably in the amount of practice they provide. Some teachers routinely practise commentary work each week; some only provide practice once or twice a year, in a mock exam.

Whatever the practice of your school, there are, in addition to what is written here, useful resources specifically written for students that will enable you to develop your skills further by yourself. A selection of these is suggested below in the bibliography. Some students find the commentary the hardest part of the programme. It should not be, provided you become familiar with how to read poems and prose extracts, and get plenty of practice. These two things: familiarity and practice, are the principal keys to success in commentary.

What is a commentary?

Many students, even teachers, do not know what a commentary is, when they begin. It is a form of essay, with an introduction, body (a clear sequence of paragraphs) and conclusion, following the norms of an essay. It could be described as:

A structured response to a prose passage or poem that:
* shows understanding of and response to content
* addresses all significant elements
* illuminates how its form and language create meaning.

It is an exercise in: understanding through close reading; in personal response; and in writing. It is a particular challenge in the exam because it is 'unseen': you are not expected to have seen the passage or poem before. You need to make sense of the text quickly, and identify important elements. As you read through this chapter, and study the samples, you will gain a clearer idea about what a commentary is and what is expected in a good performance. The assessment criteria will indicate what the examiner will be looking for in your work, but there is no one formula for writing a good commentary.

The difference between the Standard Level and Higher Commentaries

The assessment criteria for Higher and Standard Level are almost identical, differing only in a few details of wording and expectations. The main differences are that (a) the time allotted for the Standard Commentary is an hour and a half, and for the Higher, two hours; and (b) that Standard candidates are given several questions or points to consider, to help them focus on relevant aspects of the passages, while Higher candidates are expected to decide these for themselves. Standard candidates thus have to work very efficiently to read, plan and write their commentary in the time available. On the other hand, significant areas have already been selected for them.

Many Standard candidates prefer to work at the passages like Higher candidates, deciding on their own approach and structure, then checking that their plan does cover the guiding questions. This check is important, as the questions indicate central issues that should be addressed. Others follow the questions, structuring the commentary on these. In a successful commentary, such an approach can sound like a continuous piece of organized prose rather than three or four 'answers'. Either method can be effective and appropriate

The qualities looked for in a commentary

You should acquaint yourself with the detailed criteria for commentary, but the main qualities include:

- perceptive understanding of the *thought* and *feeling* in the text
- convincing *ideas* and personal *response*
- appreciation of *the effects* of the literary features
- a clearly focused, well developed argument
- detailed and persuasive references supporting the above aspects
- clear, precise and concise use of language with no significant lapses

How can I develop these skills? Can I accomplish something even shortly before the exam?

The skills you need for commentary are those you should acquire progressively in the course of studying the texts for your A1 programme. Extensive reading with alertness to how language is being used is the best preparation for commentary. Everything you do should contribute. The more strategically you study, with careful reading and note-taking, for example, the better your commentary skills become. There is plenty of advice in this Guide to show you how to do that.

For the desperate, however, you *can* make some difference at the last minute, and better late than never. You can put yourself through a kind of 'crash' course in a week or so by reading carefully through one or more of the suggested resources in the bibliography, as well as reading the suggestions in this chapter. For those with more time, the following will help considerably.

Reading a good range of literature, preferably beyond the requirements of the course. For example: good journalistic essays and articles, poetry of many kinds, short stories and novels. This will alert you to different styles, authorial 'voices', genres, and periods. This is important because on the exam the commentary passages and poems may be taken from any author, in any period. The 20th century may have predominated in recent years, but choices have also been made from earlier centuries. You should be aware of the different kinds or forms of poetry, for example, as well as some of the differences between pre-20th century novels and novels since the early 20th century. Working through one or more of the recommended books on commentary is an easy and efficient way to help you become familiar with a wide range of texts.

Reading closely and attentively, disciplining yourself to jot down your observations. This kind of quality reading and note-taking should routinely be practised on your IB texts, but the really conscientious can build a dossier, binder or journal, much as IB Art students are required to keep, of quotations and extracts with your comments, sharpening your perceptions as you go. As you do this, you should be extending your vocabulary, an important part of your skill-building.

Developing your own response and ideas. You will be assessed on these, so it's important to work at them. The kind of close reading and noting described above, along with active participation in discussion, will help. Students often think that reading is less demanding than other subjects such as math, and do it for example in bed when falling asleep. On the contrary, since it needs a creative effort on your part, it needs a fresh, concentrated mind and a well-chosen time.

Becoming familiar with literary terms and features, seeing how these work to enhance meaning and effect. 'Seeing how they work' is the key. Mere identification of terms should be avoided. You will not gain credit from the simple spotting of an example of a metaphor, but you will from being able to discuss why it is especially effective in its context and how it contributes to the total effect (See the discussion below on "The Eagle" for an example.)

You should be comfortable with many of the terms in the glossary provided, as early in the course as possible. The point of being able to use technical terms is to describe and analyse an effect more precisely. For example, to say of Robert Frost's line," Nature's first green is gold" that 'the alliteration points to an apparent paradox' is more concise than 'His use of 'g' at the beginning of two words close together points to an idea that seems to be a contradiction'.

Developing the articulation or expression of your responses and ideas, both orally and in writing. The commentary paper is as much a test of *writing* as it is of reading and understanding. Students often say that one of their biggest problems is that "I can't express my ideas". This is usually because they don't have enough opportunities to do this, whereas even a few hours' practice will begin to make a difference.

There is a connection between oral work and writing in terms of articulation. Expressing your ideas orally about what you are reading, through class participation, or, if this doesn't provide sufficient opportunity, with friends, even parents (they may surprise you with their interest in doing this), *will* help your writing. One group of students formed a lunchtime club to read and talk about poetry, and it worked for them.

Getting ideas: The kind of oral practice described above will also help you generate ideas. Students frequently say: "How can I get ideas?". The "getting of ideas" begins to come quite quickly as you engage in discussion with others. If you gain confidence expressing your ideas orally, writing will also become easier. Try writing sections of your notes in continuous prose, as illustrated on "The Eagle" and "Westminster Bridge" below, instead of the usual abbreviated notes.

How useful are strategies and checklists for analysing texts?

When you begin commentary work, it is definitely helpful to have some ideas about how to approach texts and what to look for, so strategies can be very useful at this stage. You have to start somewhere. The danger with checklists is that they are rather rigid, and may lead to a fragmented, mechanical and restricted response (because of the attempt to apply each point). Not all listed points will have relevance to every passage. What is needed is a personal response that arises from sensitivity to the *particular* qualities of a *particular* passage or poem.

The ideal is to move as quickly as possible from the stage of relying on such lists, to having the confidence to read any passage and respond to its particular meaning and distinctive qualities. Let these shape your commentary. Checklists are no substitute for sheer practice in close reading and understanding, and for developing your own capacity for response. That is why you are taken through some poems in the section that follows, rather than just provided with a list. When you are developing your skills, it's a good idea to read a commentary text several times closely, jotting down as many ideas as possible, and then to turn to the checklist to see if you have missed anything important.

Frequently Asked Questions about Commentary

Could I focus on either the poetry or the prose?
Focusing on one or the other is definitely not recommended, for several reasons. One type of commentary is not easier or more accessible than the other. Nor can you know in advance whether the prose passage or the poem will most appeal to you and permit you to demonstrate your skills to the best advantage. There is much overlap between the skills of reading and appreciating poems closely, and reading prose. However, there are some literary features that are usually more pronounced or significant in prose than in poetry, and *vice versa*. The following discussions should make this clear.

What if I miss the meaning?
This is quite a common student concern, understandably when the commentary is *'unseen'*. If you follow the stages and discussions in this chapter, and if you reinforce this with further reading, making it a frequent activity, you are unlikely to miss the significance altogether. Remember that many different elements are being assessed in this exercise, such as language, for example, and you will gain credit where it is due. If you misinterpret or neglect tone, for example, you cannot be penalized for this under 'use of language'. There are five

criteria and you can only be penalized once, in one criterion, for each weakness. This makes it a fair system!

Suppose the examiner disagrees with my interpretation?
It is true that literature is not read or responded to in exactly the same way by each reader. Your background experience, knowledge, and character tendencies, affect the way you respond to a piece of writing. You may notice and respond more strongly to this or that aspect, than another reader. From one period of history to another, emphasis in the way literature is read also changes to some extent.

However, we can say that there is a consensus of intelligent opinion about what poems and passages are about and what particular features contribute to this meaning. A poem or prose piece cannot mean absolutely anything. While you are expected to grasp a certain core of meaning and effect that most informed people would agree on, examiners are there to evaluate the quality and validity of your responses, and reward you for independent ideas if these can be persuasively stated and well supported from the text. The key here is 'evidence'. Parts of texts may be obscure or ambiguous, and your intelligent efforts to grapple with these in the light of the whole meaning will be rewarded. So, there are areas about which there cannot be much disagreement, and others that are more open to personal response. The varied criteria allow for this.

2. Reading and appreciating poetry for the commentary

Writing poetry is a common and universal and very ancient human activity. It seems to answer a need in our lives to express and share deep feelings or significant perceptions. Students often write poetry themselves, yet they equally often think of poetry as demanding and difficult to read. The following ways of approaching poetry may help. More emphasis is given to poetry than to prose in this chapter because prose is also covered in the following chapters on How to Study Texts and The Exam Essay. Many other books are devoted to helping students understand and analyse poetry in general, but this discussion bears in mind requirements and problems specific to the IB exam. There is a particular focus on aspects of commentary that candidates have trouble with year after year.

(i) The human impulse behind the poem

All poetry emanates from a human being, is a human utterance. We always need a 'point of entry' into a poem. A useful starting point is therefore to read a poem and consider what kind of human impulse lies behind it. Too often students look at poems merely as words on a page. What might have stimulated the poet to write it? Does it seem to be:

• The recapturing and shaping of a significant personal experience?
• The expression of a point of view or argument?
• An attempt to open the reader's mind to an idea or perception?
• Something else?

This should help connect you with the voice and tone and intention of the poem, which are all essential aspects to grasp. It should help you gain a *coherent reading* of the text, something which many candidates find it difficult to do. If you read it aloud, trying to convey what you think the poet is saying with the appropriate tone and pacing, you should recapture something of the impulse behind it. Listening to poetry on tape also helps a lot. Look at the following poem by Alfred Lord Tennyson, ask yourself what was the probable impulse behind it, and write this down.

The Eagle

He clasps the crag with crooked hands;
Close to the sun in lonely lands,
Ringed with the azure world he stands.

The wrinkled sea beneath him crawls;
He watches from his mountain walls,
And like a thunderbolt he falls.

The question is useful because the focus is all on the image of the bird, and we do not seem to 'hear' the narrator's personal tone or even sense his presence. But we can say that the poet seems to have been struck by the majesty and power and solitude of the eagle, which he conveys in this vivid image. That looks like the *raison d'etre,* the 'reason for being' of this poem. We will return to the poem later.

Let's turn to another well-known poem: "Composed Upon Westminster Bridge" by William Wordsworth, and consider the impulse behind this, the emotions with which he describes.

Earth has not anything to show more fair;
Dull would he be of soul who could pass by
A sight so touching in its majesty;
This city now doth like a garment, wear
The beauty of the morning; silent, bare
Ships, towers, domes, theatres, and temples, lie
Open unto the fields, and to the sky;
All bright and glittering in the smokeless air.
Never did sun more beautifully steep
In his first splendour, valley, rock or hill;
Ne're saw I, never felt, a calm so deep!
The river glideth at his own sweet will;
Dear God! The very houses seem asleep;
And all that mighty heart is lying still!

Here the impulse is much more transparent. The presence of the narrator, the poet, is strong; the time, the scene, is clear. The emotions of wonder and awe and pleasure are evident (the exclamation marks make this clear). The impulse to communicate this is obvious. In the case of both poems the focus is on a vivid image seen, that the poet recaptures in all its vividness in words, but the role of the narrator is different.

So a starting point in reading a poem can be the establishment of what the poet is essentially conveying. Read a few more poems in this way and write a sentence or two expressing the 'impulses'. Some poetry checklists begin by asking 'What is the situation?' 'Who is the speaker?' These are variations on this approach.

(ii) Tension or contrast

Many poems are built around a tension or contrast that gives them edge and interest. So a second stage can be to identify this as a way of appreciating the shape and movement of the poem. The tension may be in the form of a 'problem' that is resolved in the course of the poem, as in some of Shakespeare's sonnets. Re-read the Tennyson and the Wordsworth poems to decide how this might apply to them.

You might say that the contrast in "The Eagle" is spatial or physical: between the mountain walls 'close to the sun', and the sea so far below that waves are like wrinkles. The eagle plummets between these two points in the second stanza, illustrating his power and precision. You could develop this approach by saying that the contrast is two-fold. There is equally a contrast between stillness and movement, balanced in the two stanzas, dependent on the spatial contrast for its effect. This is an important part of the point and purpose of the poem.

In the Wordsworth poem the contrast is more implicit: between the beauty of this early moment of tranquillity and clarity (smokelessness), and the noise, movement, life (and sadly, pollution) which will return when the city wakes up. There is a 'tension' because we are aware how ephemeral or fleeting this peaceful moment is. The sleeping city will wake. But there is also the contrast and balance of urban and rural beauty. This city river scene rivals in its beauty the imagined dawn on the mountains.

There are even perhaps further contrasts, between the single awake individual, who would normally be unseen against the rush of the city, and the sleeping giant of the capital and heart

11

of the nation, paradoxically 'majestic' and 'touching'. These tensions or contrasts constitute a significant part of the meaning and effect of the poem. The poet could not have been so transfixed by the sight had he not known it was both unusual and momentary.

Tension or contrast in a poem is often a subtle matter, but if you develop a feel for it you have gone a long way to appreciating both purpose and shape as well as interest in a work. Identifying this is also an important part of prose commentary, as you will see from the student essay on *The Horse's Mouth* later.

(iii) The logic of development

Most poems contain a sequence or logic of development and you need to be able to recognize this. It may be an intricate process of thought (or argument) that winds its way through the poem, as in a John Donne poem. It may be a sequence of images or scenes, however short, like the Tennyson and Wordsworth poems, following the direction the eye moves in. The poem also may be a description of an experience, resembling a narrative.

So having looked at the poem holistically, as in stages (i) and (ii), you now need to follow the sequence carefully, line by line or stanza by stanza to see how the poem develops visually or emotionally or intellectually, or perhaps in a combination of these. A visual sequence may represent a philosophical or intellectual idea or emotion. Does the sequence, however it is represented, keep moving in one direction, or turn in an unexpected direction? "The Eagle" , for example, develops a static scene in the first five lines, then unexpectedly produces a dramatic movement in the final line.

What is the 'sequence' of the Wordsworth poem? The eye begins with the whole scene, moves over the details, then out to the edges of the city, then to imagined distant mountains, and back to the city scene, held together by a personification as a 'mighty heart'. What kind of 'meaning' does this sequence have? What part does it play in the total effect? The poet has begun with a *hyperbole* in his opening statement, expressing his surprised delight. The rest of the poem builds on this, explaining why it is so. So we might say the whole sonnet is held together by an emotional and aesthetic response, justified by the description. Look at several poems of your choice to see how they work in terms of sequence.

Remember that these elements - the impulse, the tension, the sequence - all work together to create the total effect, as do the 'features' in the next stage. We are separating them here only to make the task of analysis easier, to focus on one at a time. If you look at the assessment criteria for Commentary you will see that the first one (A) concerns understanding of the *thought and feeling* expressed in the text. The above three elements help you deal with these.

(iv) How the 'literary features', bring the main idea to life *(rhyme, rhythm, metre, diction, images, etc.)*

Criteria B and C involve interpretation, detailed analysis, and appreciation of literary features. *This is one of the weakest areas on the Commentary paper.* You can develop your skills by seeing here, and in other books on commentary, how literary features and details can be both recognized and appreciated as contributing to the whole, and how you can develop discussion of these. Look at the lines:

> He clasps the crag with crooked hands;
> Close to the sun in lonely lands,
> Ringed with the azure world he stands.

What details stand out to you (for example, individual words and phrases)? Why do they stand out? How do they seem to contribute to the central impression, or, put another way, why might the poet have chosen to use them? Can you identify them technically? (The Glossary will help here.) Remember, identifying without responding to their purpose is not enough.

Aspects that might stand out are:

- *Imagery* - The poem is primarily visual, concerned with what the poet sees and creates for us to see: 'crooked hands', 'sun', 'azure sky', 'mountain walls', 'wrinkled sea' and so on.

What part do these play in the central idea? Listing them tells us little. What is interesting is that the central subject, the eagle, is hardly described at all. The only detail is his 'crooked hands'. He 'clasps', 'stands', 'watches', 'falls' - all of which we see, but what is more important is how the imagery of his surroundings, sea and sky and mountains, enhance our sense of the power and might of the bird in these vast surroundings. It is the *qualities* of the bird, not its appearance, that the poet is concerned with. Its relationship with the surroundings is what is important. Look for the *role* of imagery in your poems. Is the imagery a starting point for the poem or does it illustrate an idea?

- **Alliteration** - the repeated 'c' in the first line. You might note that each of the alliterated words draws attention to a *visual* aspect - the crooked or gnarled foot gripping the rock - pulling these elements together. They thus reinforce the *images* referred to above. Note that alliteration can achieve many *different* effects, and that here it derives even more force from the unusual and unexpected word choice or diction.

- **Diction** - especially 'clasps' and 'crooked hands'. 'Clasps' is normally the gesture of a human, and 'hands' reinforces this idea, especially as there is only a pronoun 'he' linking the images. 'Clasps' can also suggest a regal or formal gesture, and there is a strong suggestion of the kingly or God-like nature of this creature watching from his 'mountain *walls*', 'close to the sun'. He doesn't 'grip' or 'perch'. He belongs there. 'Clasps' suggests assurance and power. However, 'crooked' is a very strong word here. Where does it fit in? Could it qualify the idea of power, suggesting a 'robber baron'? We may also note that the emphasis of these three alliterated words is *reinforced* by the metre

- **Metre** - each 'c' falls on the stressed foot of the iamb (He <u>clasps/</u> the <u>crag/</u> with <u>croo</u>/ked <u>hands</u>). Sound it out to yourself to appreciate the formality of it. The measured regularity of this line of iambic tetrameter (four metrical units) gives a kind of appropriate stateliness to the image of the bird. Sound and image work together to reinforce ideas and impressions. Think too why Tennyson should have used tetrameter, rather than a longer line like Wordsworth's iambic pentameter (five units). As it's quite a short line, it's good for crisp, clear-cut effects and statements. The longer, more flexible pentameter is good for a build up of emotional or persuasive force. Take time to figure out how these different metres contribute to the particular effect, how they work in the poems.

- **Variation of metre** - we may notice that the iambic metre (unstressed/stressed) is not adhered to rigidly, however. The variations create surprise and force, as where the stress falls on the *first* word of the second and third line ('<u>Close</u>' and '<u>Ringed</u>'). This emphasises the height and breadth of our image, taking in the sun and the expanse of the sky, and the eagle in the centre of this world.

- **Connotation** - if you try to substitute synonyms for unusual diction (choice of words) you begin to see why the poet might have made the choices he did. For example 'ringed' conveys a much sharper visual image than its synonym 'surrounded'. It also suggests royalty again, both in its sound and in its *connotation* (suggestion) of jewellery.

- **Rhyme** - why has Tennyson chosen to have each of his three-line stanzas connected by a single rhyme? It seems to suggest stateliness, control and predictability (much as the metre does). The fact that the rhyme stays the same at the end, even though the picture changes, suggests perhaps that this movement too, is part of the ordered and controlled world of the eagle. Always consider how rhyme *supports* or reinforces meaning.

- **Personification** - "The wrinkled sea beneath him crawls' is highly suggestive, striking for diction and image as much as personification. 'Wrinkled', suggests skin, but also a great height, seen from the standpoint of the eagle on his mountain walls. 'Crawls' suggests servility, lowliness, also slowness, as of some indeterminate beast. This is contrasted with the swiftness, sureness, power and calculation of the bird, qualities emphasised by the simile of the thunderbolt.

- **Simile** - The simile of the thunderbolt has overtones of Jove or Jupiter, the classical God of Thunder. Simile, like metaphor (both involve comparisons) shows the ability of the original mind to connect two normally unlike things in a particular, surprising but apt way. Always look carefully for the aptness or justice of the connection.

Enough has been discussed to show that even a tiny and seemingly simple poem can have a wealth of language features that *create the meaning* as well as the effect of the poem. The art is to integrate your separate observations, such as itemized above, into a coherent and elegant whole in an essay, showing how they work together to illustrate a central idea. Be careful to keep the main impression always in view, illuminated by techniques, not obscured by them. This kind of integration only comes with practice. Be familiar with a good number of technical terms (study the glossary) but be flexible enough to see how they work differently in each text.

A further look at some important features in poetry

Tone - One very important element in poetry that candidates often have trouble with, is *tone*. This can be a central aspect of a poem, and to miss it can lead to 'missing the meaning' and the effect of the poem. It has to do with the *attitude* of the narrator towards the subject, which might for example be bitter or compassionate. As every poem has a speaker, the voice will convey a tone that suggests feelings and attitudes about the subject. In Wordsworth's sonnet "On Westminster Bridge", his attitude to the city scene, and thus his tone, is one of delight and wonder, even rapture. These emotions inspire the writing of the poem, and run through it, binding it together. The tone is thus crucial to an understanding of this poem.

How is tone created? Although in one sense you give a poem tone by the inflections of your silent or spoken voice (nostalgic, sad, ironic, mocking, etc), on the written page you have to identify the tone through most of the elements of language: diction, rhythm, sentence construction, various sound effects, etc. For example, when Wilfred Owen writes of soldiers in the First World War as:

"Bent double, like old beggars under sacks,
Knock-kneed, coughing like hags, we cursed through sludge",

the images created by the similes and diction, the harshness of the combination of consonants, the piling up of difficult-sounding phrases conveying the physical difficulty of the march, all help convey the anger and pity the poet feels for the soldiers' experience in war.

You can help yourself define the tone of a poem by reading it aloud or hearing a recording.

Syntax - This is the grammatical structure of words in a sentence. Dull as this sounds, a slight rearrangement of the normal order of words can produce subtle and significant effects. Writers do this all the time, perhaps often unconsciously, in poetry and prose. Take Wordsworth's line in the above sonnet "On Westminster Bridge": "Dull would he be of soul who could pass by/A sight so touching in its majesty." The normal word order would be more like: "He would be dull of soul, etc." Why does he change it?

By emphasising "Dull" at the beginning of the line (with the heavy "D" sound and the stress falling on this word), he shows his pity (a touch of scorn?) for the kind of person, if such could exist, who would be unresponsive to this early morning beauty. Also, this way, the two main stress points in the line are on dull and soul, emphasised further by the consonance (the rhyming of the "l" consonants). If you moved these words close together, you would lose this clear link. Finally, it keeps the emphasis on emotions and reactions: dullness as opposed to the excitement the poet feels. If we put the vague pronoun "he" in there, the mind's eye would move to an indistinct figure, and away from appropriate feelings.

Consider too Macbeth's line in the soliloquy quoted in Chapter Four: "Upon my head they placed a fruitless crown". If you put it in the normal word order: "They placed a fruitless crown upon my head", again, something is lost. By drawing attention to himself first "*my head*", he emphasises (with bitterness and fear?) the difference between his position and Banquo's, and the irony of the whole plot of the play – he has killed for a fruitless crown. So, although his "head" is not the grammatical subject ("they", or the witches are the subject), it is very much Macbeth's subject. It is what concerns him most.

Word order, sentence structure, profoundly mirror the speaker's particular conception of his world and way of thinking. We cannot separate such effects from diction and tone, but it is important to consider them as an aspect of writing. Look at the syntax throughout "Dulce Et Decorum Est" (Chapter Four: Orals) and identify how it changes and why.

For richer awareness of the various techniques found in poetry, turn to the glossary at the end of this Guide.

****

We should now look at an example from a past IB paper and think how to approach it. Study the text carefully, using the strategies suggested below the poem, the ideas you have just read, or others that work for you.

Sample of IB Poetry Commentary (Higher Level, May 1998)

The Black Lace Fan My Mother Gave Me

It was the first gift he ever gave her,
buying it for five francs in the Galeries
in pre-war Paris. It was stifling.
A starless drought made the nights stormy.

They stayed in the city for the summer.
They met in cafés. She was always early.
He was late. That evening he was later.
They wrapped the fan. He looked at his watch.

She looked down the Boulevard des Capucines.
She ordered more coffee. She stood up.
The streets were emptying. The heat was killing.
She thought the distance smelled of rain and lightning.

These are wild roses, appliquéd on silk by hand,
darkly picked, stitched boldly, quickly.
The rest is tortoiseshell and has the reticent
clear patience of its element. It is

a worn-out, underwater bullion and it keeps,
even now, an inference of its violation.
The lace is overcast as if the weather
it opened for and offset had entered it.

The past is an empty café terrace.
An airless dusk before thunder. A man running.
And no way now to know what happened then
None at all – unless, of course, you improvise:

The blackbird on this first sultry morning,
In summer, finding buds, worms, fruit,
Feels the heat. Suddenly she puts out her wing-
The whole, flirtatious span of it.

Eavan Bolland *Outside History* (1990)

Planning a response
(This should take you twenty minutes to half an hour. Make notes on the text itself)

- Read it several times quite quickly but attentively to get a feel for what it's about.

- Make sure you read any notes or information provided on the poet or work, usually at the end of the passage. These may give you important clues (for example, about the period it was written in) that may affect your approach to the work.

- Ask questions of the text if necessary. *'Interrogate* it' as one student put it, addressing what seems difficult or unclear. By asking questions, you move nearer to answers. But remember, you can't always be certain. It is acceptable to present alternative interpretations or to express some doubt (*"This could mean…"*).

- Look for a unifying principle, central meaning, argument or impression. In other words, deal with the *whole* first. Stages (i) - (iii) above may help you here, but it is best to start with your *own* particular response to a particular text. You can go back to the strategy later.

- Now note what *features* stand out especially. You can think about how they work and contribute to the effect at the next stage, but first impressions are important.

- Read it through again carefully noting details: key words, striking diction, images, patterns, thinking about how these relate to your main idea. Make sure you have covered all parts of your text. Don't leave out a tricky stanza or section. At this point you can think about strategies and features you have read about, to be sure you don't miss anything important.

- Make a brief plan or outline. Two to three main ideas or divisions will bring coherence to the mass of ideas and details, but, as illustrated in the following section, allows you to include these. The section after that, on writing the commentary, addresses the question of what structural principle to follow.

Remember, you are not expected to be exhaustive, but you should aim to cover all *significant* aspects. You may develop, or be taught, an approach that works better for you. For example, using an acronym like SILS (subject, ideas, language, sound). There is no one ideal formula.

A student response to "The Black Lace Fan"

(To give yourself practice, make sure you have worked through it first in your chosen way; then compare with this student response)

What it's about/subject: The narrator is reconstructing as far as possible the romantic story of the fan as a gift to her mother. The appearance of the fan as she looks at it in the present seems to suggest the nature of the relationship and helps her speculate on what may have happened.

Problems/questions: Who is the man? Did he become the narrator's father? Did the couple marry? Why the mystery? Does it matter? The fourth stanza is difficult. In what sense are the wild roses 'darkly picked'? What's the significance of the strong word 'violation' in stanza five? How does the blackbird relate to the story?

Unifying principle: The fan as central object and symbol – several stages of its history - linking past and present. The fascination of history as imagination as well as fact. Opposition of known and unknown.

Striking features:
- Pronouns for the central characters. Effect?
- Setting (Paris, pre-war)
- Punctuation. Short sentences in places. Stops in mid-line (caesura). Enjambement.
- Stanza arrangement
- Weather. Symbolic?
- The narrative technique. Story interrupted and then picked up. Why? Past and present alternated.
- Diction surrounding fan ('darkly', 'boldly' etc.)
- The blackbird image
- The role of the narrator (no "I" throughout)

Details (omitted here because they appear in the essay printed below.)

16

Organization/plan: based on the *fan* as central image and the sequence of the poem
- Narration of the background and evening of the buying of the fan (include: separation of characters, weather, setting, punctuation, mood)
- The significance of the description of the fan (include: diction, connotation, image)
- The relationship of the blackbird and the fan – mood of the ending

Note that this three-step plan groups all the features listed above. These will be developed in detail in the essay.

3. Writing the Commentary

How should I organize the commentary? In a: 'linear' or 'thematic way', or by some other principle?

Students often ask this question. There is no one way that is right. As the IB is *international* it embraces different approaches. The French, the Germans, the British, the Americans, and so on, may have somewhat different methods, but the commentaries are all assessed according to the same criteria.

The structure of your commentary will be determined to a large extent by the characteristics of the poem or passage itself. Is this a tightly developed poem or passage with an argument or sequence of events? This may require a disciplined 'linear' commentary following the argument or sequence stanza by stanza or paragraph by paragraph. Or is it a passage characterized by several areas of significance, for example: content; description; chronology; contrasts; which might best be treated accordingly, in 'chunks' or sections? Perhaps the 'linear' and 'chunks' approaches can be merged to some extent, as in the student sample commentaries on "The Black Lace Fan" and *The Horse's Mouth* that follow.

The linear approach is often used and can be very effective, but a plodding, line by line analysis needs to be avoided. The difference between the effectively linear and the plodding is one of engagement and imagination. If you enter into the life of the passage/poem, understanding it, as it were, from the inside, it is unlikely you will plod. Sometimes when students read examples of a linear treatment, they think that it is just paraphrase. But description of content, response to the content, and interpretation can be intertwined.

A related question is: *If I use the linear approach, should I discuss techniques as I go along, or deal with the meaning first and then add further paragraphs on important literary features?* Because meaning and language are so closely intertwined, especially in poetry, it is often necessary to describe the content by interpreting the language. It is possible, having dealt with the development of the poem's idea (which may involve several paragraphs), to expand on some of the significant effects in subsequent paragraphs, but beware of 'tacking on' bits in a non-integrated way.

Should I give my commentary a title?

There is no need to do this (though it seems that some teachers suggest that their students should provide one) and no credit is given for the practice.

What should go into the introduction?

There is no one formula for a successful introduction. However, your introduction should make it clear that you have understood the significance of the passage or poem as a whole, and have found some *unifying principle* in it (an object, an experience, an emotion, a technique) that gives structure and focus. It can also indicate some of the ways in which you are going to develop your commentary, which often means pointing to salient literary features. Here is an example of a 'minimal' introduction.

> In his poem "The Heron", Vernon Watkins describes the striking sight of a heron standing on a rock by the sea. Through his descriptive images, metaphors, alliteration, complex rhyme scheme, and

suggestions of Greek mythology and the Bible, Watkins gives the bird almost epic significance, completely transforming this simple occurrence. (H Level, May 1997)

Here the candidate shows grasp both of the surface content of the poem (the sight of the heron by the sea), *and* of the poet's individual, transforming vision that provides the 'meaning' and interest of the poem (the 'epic significance' of the bird). It is this perception of the 'transforming vision' that makes this commentary good rather than merely satisfactory. In the second sentence he identifies literary techniques that specifically in this case help create both the meaning and the effect of the poem. Many candidates vaguely refer to 'language' rather than identifying the techniques that specifically characterize the chosen text. He is now set to show how this is accomplished, in the body of his essay.

Sometimes students successfully begin with a generalising statement that relates closely to and leads into the commentary. The key here is the *close relation* to the passage.

An object that was once an expression of love – a letter, an item of clothing, a fan - means something special to the person who received it, but may gain an additional significance with time, meaning something special to the person who inherits it too. The passage of time brings mystery and fascination. In Eavan Bolland's poem, "The Black Lace Fan my Mother Gave Me", she recreates dramatically the elusive circumstances in which the fan was bought for her mother, and seeks to reconstruct the personal 'history' she only partly knows, by pondering the fan in the present moment. Weather, punctuation and diction, among other features, bring alive past and present, linked by the fan. (H. Level, May 1998).

This introduction is more detailed than the previous one because the structure of the poem is more complex, falling into two parts.

Students ask: *What if I know the author or the work? Can I bring my knowledge in?* It is not common for this to happen, but the answer is, *if* 'outside' knowledge helps illuminate the passage and doesn't merely draw attention to your reading experience. There is a danger though, that in knowing the whole text, or other works by the same author, and seeing the passage in that wider context, some sharpness of focus on the selected passage may be lost. Consider the following, which begins with a quote from the passage:

"There's no woman anywhere around that knows as much business as you do, and we're proud of that, but of course, the real work always fell on us". Willa Catha's 1913 novel " O Pioneers!" aims to capture the effects of the late 19th century land rushes in the unsettled territories of the United States on women, using strong characterization exposed through dialogue. Like her other novels, Catha uses her writing to depict the struggle for land as well as power. (H Level May 2001)

The quote loses some effectiveness as an opening because it is separated from its context and doesn't bear much meaning on its own. It even seems to contradict the statement made in the next sentence. The 'knowledge' shown here tends to take the attention away from the specific situation in the passage which describes a competent woman asserting her rights of land over her less competent brothers. The identification of 'strong characterization exposed through dialogue' is however very apt.

Remember, it is one thing to show how a passage contributes to the whole, as you should do in your detailed study for the formal oral commentary, and another to examine a passage as an entity, with its own coherence, as you are asked to in unseen commentary.

Sample student essay on "The Black Lace Fan My Mother Gave Me"

An object that was once an expression of love – a letter, an item of clothing, a fan – meant something special to the person who received it, but may gain an additional and different significance with time for the person who inherits it. The passage of time brings mystery and fascination. In Eavan Bolland's poem the narrator recreates dramatically the elusive circumstances in which the fan was given to her mother, and seeks to reconstruct the personal history she only partly knows, by pondering the fan in the present moment. Weather, punctuation, diction, among other features, bring alive past and present, linked by the fan.

The first three stanzas move rapidly and dramatically (like the relationship itself) to the point at which the fan is to be given. The romantic but suspenseful setting of summer in 'pre-war Paris' is charged with an intensity through references to heat, starlessness and stormy nights. The tension is accentuated by the short sentences and the caesurae. "They met in cafes. She was always early / He was late. That evening he was later'. The use of the comparative 'later' there feels ominous. Bolland makes the characters mysterious and distant, more romantic and remote, by only referring to them by pronouns. She builds suspense by separating the figures with an omniscient viewpoint, moving our awareness, as in a film, between him looking at his watch in the shop, and her, waiting anxiously in a café, while the streets are emptying and the distance 'smells of rain and lightening', which seems to carry with it a sense of impending war and danger.

At this critical moment the poet breaks the narrative off to contemplate the fan. This is tantalising but effective. It creates suspense but also the description, especially the diction and images, seems to link with and build on the impression that has created about this intense, perhaps passionate relationship. 'Wild roses' suggests the spontaneity of love; the appliquéd work 'on silk' suggests not just the care and intricacy of the handiwork, but a sensuousness in the relationship. 'Darkly picked, stitched boldly, quickly' could relate to the sense of fervour, speed, risk of the relationship in these times, yet is at odds with the delicacy of the idea of appliqué work, and cannot be interpreted literally. Nature and art (quickly picked wild roses and appliquéd embroidery) merge.

The tortoiseshell handle of the fan is by contrast, sturdy. It resists time (like gold or bullion) even more than the lace and embroidery, like the quiet long-lived turtle in its watery element. Does patience relate to an element of this relationship? Did 'she' have to wait for 'him' because of the war? The 'overcast' lace is a strikingly tactile link between past and present. The weather of that moment seems to have penetrated the fabric, bringing sharply into the present that far-off evening. We assume, because it was 'opened' and 'offset the weather', and because the fan has lived on, that he reached her. The narrator can touch and smell that fabric that her mother touched years ago.

But the narrative collapses or disintegrates at this point. Cryptic and ominous images of the 'empty café terrace', 'dusk before thunder', 'a man running', pick up the suspense of the earlier part of the narrative, but then like a film still, transfix this moment in time forever, the space between the lovers seemingly eternal. Where the narrative of the first three stanzas was precise in its detail, with its 'five francs in the Galeries' and the ordering of more coffee, knowledge here peters out. But the poet narrator needs to finish her story, needs to make the link between the man running, and the gift that was given, the 'first' of a number. Like any historian, she has to guess, follow a hunch, improvise, use her imagination. A real blackbird, presumably in her garden in the present moment of early summer (sultry, but not 'stifling') supplies the idea. Protecting herself against the heat, the bird spreads her wing like a fan, ' the whole flirtatious span of it', as the narrator's mother must have done on receiving the fan, the beginning of a new stage in the relationship.

Did 'he' marry 'her', or was this a wartime relationship? Is he the father of the narrator? The mystery is an important element in the effect of the poem, which haunts with its fragments, and the tautness of its telling. This is an effective choice of the poet/narrator, who might have chosen to put herself in the foreground and explore her own feelings about the fan and the past but instead, keeps herself out of the picture, focusing on the story. The poem is somehow satisfying in its resolution, suggesting the renewal of life and connecting past and present positively.

Comments on the sample essay

This is a 'linear' reading, which is appropriate because the poem develops a narrative that is suggestive rather than explicit and needs to be interpreted. However, there is a clear structure, as indicated in the plan outlined earlier. In this, the candidate makes clear that he will be basing his commentary on the three stages he has identified in the narrative, and will focus on different features in each of these. Thus, interpretation of content and discussion of features are woven together and parts are clearly related to the whole. Ambiguities and mysteries are addressed, but not necessarily resolved.

4. Reading and Appreciating Prose Commentary

A prose passage may seem easier to read than a poem. The language and meaning are usually more transparent, less dense or concentrated in effect. But what to look for and how to appreciate features is just as hard. Unlike poems, where the whole text is usually provided and you are looking for the whole meaning and effect, prose passages are usually taken from a longer work. However, they will be chosen as having coherence and significance in themselves and this is what you will focus on.

Literary features in prose: strategies for approaching prose commentary

You will see that there is a certain overlap with the features of poetry, but other features are more important than is typical in poetry, such as the role of the narrator, the point of view, and the chronology. Read the following in conjunction with the discussion in the next two chapters on How to Study Texts and The Examination Essay. The following questions should also help in guiding you to read attentively for all of your assessed components including the oral.

What is the passage about? What is the focus? Is it about an event and what that reveals, a decision a character makes, a character's circumstances, or something else? Define this in a sentence or two.

Who is narrating this passage? Is there a first person ("I") narrator, or third person (often called omniscient)? You may need to distinguish between the narrator and the author or creator of the narrator. What attitude does the narrator have towards his/her subject? (Look at irony later in this list). How might we describe the tone of narration? What attitude do we seem encouraged to take towards the narrator? (ie: How does the author manipulate his creation, the narrator? *The Horse's Mouth*, provided below is a good example). Is there a shift in narrator or point of view during the passage?

Is there a central character or group of characters? What do we learn about him/her/them? How do we learn these things? Through dialogue, description, interior monologue, or other devices?

How is the passage structured? Does it fall into distinct sections? What characterises these? What rationale does the structure have? (Different stages of a journey, of an experience, or a thought process, or something else?)

Is the development chronological? Is the passage narrated strictly in sequence, or does it look backwards or forwards at any point? Is knowledge withheld and then revealed strategically? (Look at how this is done in the prose commentary following).

What tensions or oppositions or contrasts are evident? Within a character? Between characters? Between the external world and a character? In the *Frankenstein* passage below, there is a contrast between the scientist indoors, and the world beyond his window.

What part does description or setting play? Does it reflect a character's thoughts and attitudes, provide a contrast to what is happening in the character's mind, create suspense or atmosphere, or something else? What senses does it appeal to?

What language effects are striking? Is the diction memorable? Are there patterns of words? Are metaphors and similes or symbols used? What part do they play? Are sound effects prominent at any point? Does the level of language shift, for example from colloquial or slang to a more literary level?

What tense and mood is used? Is past, present or another tense employed? To what effect? Is the mood indicative ('You arrive at the station'), interrogative ('Can you buy a ticket?'), imperative ('Step onto the platform')? If so, what impact does this have on a reader?

Are there particular effects created by punctuation, syntax or sentence structure? Short or long sentences? Do these reflect what is happening in the narrative?

Is dialogue used? Does this provide characterisation? Does it work dramatically, representing 'events' or movement in the plot as in the *Pride and Prejudice* extract in Chapter Two: How to Study Texts? Does it introduce a theme, like marriage?

If this is the beginning of a work, how successful do you think it is as such? What characteristics does it establish about the work?

How are we being invited to read the passage? With sympathy for the main character? With a critical distance from him/her? Both? This can be related to irony.

Is irony present? (ie: a gap between what is said, and how we are intended to take it) This is a very frequent effect in prose. Is the irony *stylistic*, where a statement is made that we are not intended to take at face value (see Chapter Two, *Pride and Prejudice*). Or is it '*dramatic*', where the reader is presented with facts that are at odds with the character's understanding of a situation. In other words, with a superior understanding provided by the narrator / author, as in *The Horse's Mouth*, below.

What kind of effect does the passage have on you? Does it challenge your ideas? Open you to new perspectives? Engage you by presenting a suspenseful and dramatic situation, or with a character or characters in whom you take an interest?

Sample of IB Prose Commentary (Higher Level May 1997): *The Horse's Mouth*

Work through the passage first for a general effect, then with the above questions in mind, and lastly compare your ideas and plan with the student sample that follows.

I was walking by the Thames. Half-past morning on an autumn day. Sun in a mist. Like an orange in a fried-fish shop. All bright below. Low tide, dusty water and a crooked bar of straw, chicken boxes, dirt and oil from mud to mud. Like a viper swimming in skim milk. The old serpent, symbol of nature and love.

> Five windows light the caverned man; through one he breathes the air.
> Through one he hears music of the spheres; through one can look
> And see small portions of the eternal world.(1)

Such as Thames mud turned into a bank of nine carat gold rough from the fire. They say a chap just out of prison runs into the nearest cover; into some dark little room, like a rabbit put up by a stoat. The sky feels too big for him. But I liked it. I swam in it. I couldn't take my eyes off the clouds, the water, the mud. And I must have been hopping up and down Greenbank Hard for half an hour grinning like a gargoyle, until the wind began to get up my trousers and down my back, and to bring me to myself, as they say. Meaning my liver and lights. (2)

And I perceived that I hadn't time to waste on pleasure. A man of my age has got to get on with the job.

I had two and six left from my prison money. I reckoned that five pounds would set me up with bed, board and working capital. That left four pounds seventeen and sixpence to be won. From friends. But when I went over my friends, I seemed to owe them more than that; more than they could afford.

The sun had crackled into flames at the top; the mist was getting thin in places, you could see the crooked lines of grey, like old cracks under spring ice. Tide on the turn. Snake broken up. Emeralds and sapphires. Water like varnish with bits of gold leaf floating thick and heavy. Gold is the metal of intellect. And all at once the sun burned through in a new place, at the side, and shot out a ray that hit the Eagle and Child (3), next to the motor-boat factory, right on the new signboard.

A sign, I thought. I'll try my old friend Coker. Must start somewhere. Coker, so I heard, was in trouble. But I was in trouble and people in trouble, they say, are more likely to give help to each other than those who aren't. After all, it's not surprising, for people who help each other in trouble are likely soon to be in trouble themselves. And then, they are generally people who enjoy the consolation of other people's troubles. Sympathetic people. Who'd rather see each other's tears, boo-hoo, than the smile of a millionaire, painted in butter on a barber's shave.

Coker kept the public bar at the Eagle. About five foot high and three foot broad. Face like a mule, except the eyes, which are small and blue. Methylated. The Eagle is down on Thames-side and gets some rough ones. But see little Coker run a six-foot pug through the door, by the scruff and the seat, his ears throwing off sparks like new horseshoes. Coker has a small hand, but it feels like hot marbles. Coker has had a hard life. Long-bodied and short-tempered.

There were three chaps hanging around the door for the bar to open, and I asked 'em "Is it true about Coker?" But they were strangers. Come up on an empty gravel barge. They didn't know Coker. Just then I saw her coming along with a string-bag full of knitting and her slippers. Snugs for the snug (4). I smiled and raised my hat, took it right off.

"Hullo, Coker. So here we are again".

"So you're out are you? Thought it was tomorrow".

"I'm out Coker. And glad to see you. I suppose there aren't any letters for me?"

"Have you come to pay me my money", said Coker, with a look that made me step back a pace. "That's all right", I said quickly. "I'll pay you Coker, I couldn't do anything about it while I was inside, could I?"

"As if you ever did. But you won't get any more".

"I wouldn't think of it, Coker'.

But Coker was getting fiercer and fiercer. Working herself up. She squared at me as if she meant to give me a knock. And I took another step back.

"What about that lawyer of yours that was bringing a case? You told a lot of people. I should think they'll all want their money back now you're out again.

"You'll get your money back, Coker, with interest".

"Yes, I'm going to", and she put the key in the door. "Four pounds fourteen. I'm going to see about it Wednesday. And you're coming with me; to see that woman who's giving the evidence. And if you're having us on, it looks like another police job."

The three chaps were looking, but what did Coker care. I like Coker. She doesn't give a curse.

****

From Joyce Carey, opening of The Horse's Mouth (5) *(the story of an artist, and his adventures both in art and life, told by himself). (1944)*

Footnotes
  1. *from* 'Europe and Prophecy' 1794, by William Blake, poet and artist
  2. liver and lights: entrails from lights=lungs(colloquial)
  3. a Public House= a bar
  4. snug = small bar for select customers
  5. the horse's mouth= authentic source of information (proverbial)

Sample student essay on the prose commentary: *The Horse's Mouth*

The short, rather laconically matter-of-fact sentence, "I was walking by the Thames" seems an unlikely beginning for a novel. However, a few sentences into the opening extract of The Horse's Mouth *quickly dispels this view. The passage continues in the unusual vein of the first sentence, both linguistically and thematically, juxtaposing slang with literary quotations, mundane city-bred images with bizarre similes, and an artistic, erudite man with a criminal record. This extract, marked by its startling diction and language, is also notable for the method of character delineation used. The first person narrative prevents the use of direct description to elucidate the protagonist's personality. Instead, through the speaker's use of language and his uncommon attitude towards the world in general and Coker in particular, we gather much about him. Coker too is described in such a way that the simple fact she is a woman comes as a surprise. The image of a tough public bar keeper carrying her knitting shows a keen understanding of the irony of city life as well as describing Coker vividly. This piece is rife with irony and surreal juxtapositions that together combine to create a vibrant picture of the protagonist, his 'friend' Coker and their environment, thus setting the scene for the novel's action.*

The passage describes the situation of a man who has just been released from prison. We find him admiring the river Thames in autumn, reflecting on the beauty of the outside world after his period of incarceration. He then returns to more practical considerations, running through his list of friends to find one who would be willing to lend him money. With some guidance from a stray ray of sunlight, which he interprets as a sign, he decides on Coker, the public house keeper, who is rumoured to be in trouble herself. When he does go to see her, she fiercely demands that he repay his debt to her, and the narrator, instead of resenting this, seems to like her all the more for her aggression.

The first person narrative is almost confessional, and reads much like a personal diary. The fragmented sentences and uneven paragraph lengths and spacing further add to this impression. The short phrases have an immediacy that draws the reader in without the preliminary niceties of scene setting. Very quickly, almost like a sketch, the narrator gives the time and place of the story and then adds the powerful image of the "sun in a mist. Like an orange in a fried-fish shop" which forms the focus of the scene being described. The simile is peculiarly apt because of the way it immediately evokes the city of London. The speaker then piles on image upon image of the river Thames using short, staccato sentences that add to the cinematic surreal quality of the language. There is a strong correlation between the diction used and the thematic purpose of the writer. The speaker is reflecting on the sensual pleasure of sight after his long deprivation of it while in prison. The strongly visual language and the well-chosen quotation from Blake's 'Europe and Prophecy' support this. He then rouses himself from his reflections, realizing that he "hadn't time to waste on pleasure". Similarly, when the speaker breaks out of his trance and returns to more practical matters, he uses everyday language and even slang to signal his change of mood: " the wind began to... bring me back to myself, as they say. Meaning my liver and lights".

The use of literary, mythological and religious allusions serves not only to enrich the fanciful, descriptive language but also to demonstrate the speaker's erudition. His easy familiarity with Blake, himself an artist and poet, may lead one to surmise that perhaps Blake is an inspiration for and influence on him. Such titbits of knowledge help in creating a composite, credible picture of the speaker as a real character with personal role models and heroes. The image of the speaker grinning like the mythical gargoyle, while humorous, is also unusual, in keeping with the linguistic theme of odd similes and metaphors. The rather cryptic non-sequitur "Gold is the metal of the intellect" may also be a mythological allusion, perhaps referring to the alchemist's search for the philosopher's stone that would turn ordinary metals to gold

Religious allusions are used liberally, including the recurring image of the snake, "symbol of love and nature" and also of temptation (relevant perhaps for a man just coming out of prison). The so-called sign that leads the speaker to Coker also seems religious, resonating with the idea of burning bushes and similar revelation-inducing guides. It is reminiscent of Raskolnikov's superstitious interpretation of the events leading up to the murder in Dostoyevsky's Crime and Punishment. Raskolnikov believes that the chance event which allows him to learn of the most opportune time of committing the murder, after he had decided not to go ahead with it, is a sign of fate. Though this speaker lacks Raskolnikov's morbidity, one wonders whether the religious allusions may not signal a future moral dilemma in the speaker's life, or if it may be symptomatic of his own grappling with religion. In this light, the fact that he quotes Blake, who was known as a mystic and created his own religious myths, becomes even more significant and allows further speculation about the narrator's personality.

The last part of the passage is more dynamic than the first. Dialogue, action and the first element of tension emerges through the interaction of Coker and the narrator. The idea of Coker and the narrator flocking together as people in trouble is an endearingly optimistic one on the part of the speaker. The early description of Coker as a tough pub-keeper combined with the use of a surname to refer to her created the impression that she was male. When we realize she is female (with the ridiculous introduction of a knitting bag) it is almost as if the author has played a joke on us by allowing us to jump to strictly gendered conclusions. Another feature which stand out in the description of Coker is that of her eyes. The narrator uses the single word "Methylated" to evoke the clarity and purity of colour of her eyes. Coker's speech, rough and colloquial, completes the picture of the city-bred survivor, a fighter who should be respected for her spirit, as the speaker has the wit to realize. The idea of the narrator liking Coker even after she curses him and threatens police action against him seems somehow contradictory. However, it shows his sensitivity in recognising strength in another when he sees it. It also softens Coker, making her seem a more sympathetic character than her actions seem to justify.

Thus, in conclusion, this piece relies on the juxtaposition of contradictory attitudes and qualities to create real, quirky and somehow likeable characters, and to build a surreal picture of London. The author achieves this, however, without hiding the facts of the poverty and dirt of city life, and the flaws and rough edges of characters created in part by the hardships of this life.

Comments on the sample

The candidate packs a lot into her introduction (you may feel it is *too* detailed). She clearly identifies many significant areas of style and content, and her final sentence in the first paragraph shows excellent sense of the focus of the passage. Already in the introduction there is considerable awareness of literary features: of style and language, of narrator and characterization, of chronology and surprise. The language is confident and the vocabulary varied and effective.

The second paragraph provides a concise, interpretive summary, showing she has grasped the content well. This leaves her free to focus in detail later on aspects of the piece without having to constantly make the narrative line clear or proceed in a rigidly linear way. It is surprising how many candidates don't grasp the content clearly.

The next paragraph, dealing with the description of the Thames, is sensitive to punctuation, sentence structure and style, but is a little disappointing in not saying rather more about the vivid and unusual images of the Thames and particularly that these perceptions seem to be those of an *artist*. (The notes at the end of the passage helpfully reveal that the narrator was an artist. This is a good example of where such notes can affect your reading of the whole passage. Candidates quite often fail to pay attention to such notes.) Even the best commentaries are rarely if ever perfect, however, and such flaws or omissions should not blind us to how much is accomplished here. This is, after all, an *unseen* exam.

She then takes on the challenge of the allusions with an intelligent and speculative approach. She makes an analogy with *Crime and Punishment*. If such references genuinely occur to the candidate and illuminate or clarify the passage, they may be acceptable, but should be used with restraint, in passing, as it were. They should not be deliberately sought or strained for and should certainly not become dominant in the discussion: the focus must remain clearly on the passage. No aspect of the assessment criteria *specifically* rewards such analogies (though an illuminating idea will be rewarded under Criterion B).

There are some excellent insights about the narrator and Coker in the penultimate paragraph, and some implicit awareness of the irony of the presentation of the narrator here, where action takes over and he is no longer 'in control'. The conclusion brings ideas together with a fine focus and goes further, sharpening some insights about the whole passage (the contrasts and the quirky likeableness of the characters, for example). The candidate has expanded the reader's understanding and appreciation of the passage through her own fine grasp of it, which is what a good commentary should do.

5. Standard Level Commentary

The following passage is good practice for Higher Level candidates as well as Standard, particularly in the early stages of developing commentary skills. Similarly, Standard candidates should work through the Higher Level samples and comments for more guidance and practice.

How to use the guiding questions

Standard Level poems and passages are accompanied by guiding questions. Because of this, students often ask: should I just focus on answering the questions, or can I structure my commentary in my own way? The answer is that you can do either, provided you address all the significant features, as has been discussed above. If you base your commentary on the questions, this should be done in such a way that the commentary reads in a smooth and structured way, addressing all the significant aspects of the passage. The danger with merely answering the questions is that you do not sufficiently develop your own responses and ideas.

If you take the more holistic approach, deciding first on what you think is significant, you should still consult the questions and ensure that they are addressed somewhere in your essay. They are intended to point to areas of particular significance and it would be unwise not to consider them. In addition, you don't have a lot of time (just an hour and a half) and need to work efficiently. The questions ensure that you identify some of the crucial aspects quickly.

Sample of IB prose commentary (Standard Level, May 1999) *Frankenstein*

Read through the following passage from Mary Shelley's <u>Frankenstein</u> *at least twice, deciding on what you think are the most striking elements and sketching quickly some ideas and details you would want to include. Then consult the questions following the passage, to see if you have omitted anything important. You might also want to look back at the list of prose features (p.20-21), for more ideas. Decide which of the structural approaches discussed above would work best for you.*

I sat one evening in my laboratory; the sun had set, and the moon was just rising from the sea; I had not sufficient light for my employment, and I remained idle, in a pause of consideration of whether I should leave my labour for the night, or hasten its conclusion by an unremitting attention to it. As I sat, a train of reflection occurred to me, which led me to consider the effects of what I was now doing. Three years before, I was engaged in the same manner, and had created a fiend whose unparalleled barbarity had desolated my heart, and filled it forever with the bitterest remorse. I was now about to form another being, of whose disposition I was alike ignorant; she might become ten thousand times more malignant than her mate, and delight, for its own sake, in murder and wretchedness. He had sworn to quit the neighbourhood of man, and hide himself in deserts; but she had not, and she, who in all probability was to become a thinking and reasoning animal, might refuse to comply with a compact made before her creation. They might even hate each other; the creature who already lived, loathed his own deformity, and might he not conceive a greater abhorrence for it when it came before his eyes in the female form? She also might turn in disgust from him to the superior beauty of man; she might quit him, and he be alone again, exasperated by the fresh provocation of being deserted by one of his own species.

Even if they were to leave Europe, and inhabit the deserts of the new world, yet one of the first results of those sympathies for which the demon thirsted would be children, and a race of devils would be propagated on earth who might make the very existence of the species of man a condition precarious and full of terror. Had I a right, for my own benefit, to inflict this curse upon everlasting generations? I had before been moved by the sophisms (1) of the being I had created; I had been struck senseless by his fiendish threats: but now, for the first time, the wickedness of my promise burst upon me; I shuddered to think that future ages might curse me as their pest, whose selfishness had not hesitated to buy its own peace at the price perhaps of the existence of the whole human race.

I trembled, and my heart failed within me; when, on looking up, I saw, by the light of the moon, the daemon at the casement. A ghastly grin wrinkled his lips as he gazed on me, where I sat fulfilling the task which he had allotted to me. Yes, he had followed me in my travels; he had loitered in forests, hid himself in caves, or taken refuge in wide and desert heaths; and he now came to mark my progress, and claim the fulfilment of my promise.

As I looked on him, his countenance expressed the utmost extent of malice and treachery. I thought with a sensation of madness on my promise of creating another like to him, and trembling with passion, tore to pieces the thing on which I was engaged. The wretch saw me destroy the creature on whose future existence he depended for happiness, and with a howl of devilish despair and revenge, withdrew.

I left the room, and, locking the door, made a solemn vow in my own heart never to resume my labours; and then, with trembling steps, I sought my own apartment. I was alone; none were near me to dissipate the gloom, and relieve me from the sickening oppression of the most terrible reveries.

Several hours passed, and I remained near my window gazing on the sea; it was almost motionless, for the winds were hushed, and all nature reposed under the eye of the quiet moon. A few fishing vessels alone specked the water, and now and then the gentle breeze wafted the sound of voices, as the fishermen called to one another. I felt the silence, although I was hardly conscious of its extreme profundity, until my ear was suddenly arrested by the paddling of oars near the shore, and a person landed close to my house.

In a few minutes after, I heard the creaking of my door, as if someone endeavoured to open it softly. I trembled from head to foot; I felt a presentiment of who it was, and wished to rouse one of the peasants who dwelt in a cottage not far from mine; but I was overcome by the sensation of helplessness.

Mary Wollstonecraft Shelley
Frankenstein; or *The Modern Prometheus* (2) (1818)

1. apparently attractive arguments
2. in Greek mythology, the demi-god who stole fire from heaven and gave it back to man, for which he was punished by Zeus.

- What do the details of the setting contribute to the effects of the passage?
- What characteristics and powers might Frankenstein's female creation have possessed?
- How and to what effect does Shelley introduce the daemon (monster) into the passage?
- What is the effect of the tone and content given here to Victor Frankenstein's narrative?

Before reading on, construct your own response to the passage as suggested above.

Student response to the passage: towards an essay plan

First reading:

I read the passage through carefully and came up with three words that I felt summed up the most striking effects – 'horror', 'fear', and 'isolation'. I thought 'horror' because this expresses what Frankenstein has suffered in these three years and what might happen as a result of his creation in the future, which he vividly imagines with dread. 'Fear' is created by the sense of the daemon pursuing him and menacing him. 'Isolation' describes the scientist alone in his laboratory, alone in his terrifying thoughts and dilemma, and again alone in his apartment later.

Second reading:

This time I went carefully through the text in a linear way noting my impressions and ideas, as follows. (I enlarge my notes here so that they can be followed more easily.)

- The opening seems calm and rational as Frankenstein introduces us to his immediate situation in formal language ("in a pause of consideration", " hasten its conclusion", etc.). The approaching night seems peaceful rather than sinister.
- Line 6 unexpectedly, with superlatives and strong diction, contrasting with the above, expresses the reality of his situation ("fiend", "unparalleled barbarity", "desolated my heart", "bitterest remorse").
- He speculates with horror about what the new creature might be like, and what she might do, and how the two fiends might react to one another. We live through his appalled train of thought with him, the unknown element emphasized by the question "Might he not...?"
- The second paragraph continues the speculation, but widens the field to include the idea of 'offspring' that could terrorize mankind. At the centre of the paragraph and the passage, comes the critical ethical question he must answer and act upon. Can he justify (by creating the new fiend) imperilling mankind for his own benefit, his peace of existence?
- We see his emotional state ("I trembled and my heart failed")
- The train of thought has so engrossed the scientist and us that the appearance of the daemon at the window takes us by surprise. The syntax aids this. We see the moonlight first, then the daemon, made more horrible by the light. The only precise details are the moonlight and the "ghastly grin" on his "wrinkled lips" but they are enough to suggest the horror of the whole. There is a sense that Frankenstein is trapped, in the power of the fiend. We identify with the situation of this first person narrator.
- Lines 35 - 36 form a climax as he answers his question with a passionate and dramatic action, and tears up his new creation, watched by the fiend. The strong diction relating to the fiend suggest the consequences of such action: "malice and treachery", "devilish despair and revenge", and create fear in us as we witness this along with Frankenstein.
- Frankenstein's emotional isolation is stressed ("I was alone; none were near me...")
- The focus of attention passes to the tranquillity of the seascape outside his apartment window. This lulls us, and again, we are taken by surprise as he hears "a person" land close to his house.
- Aural imagery builds suspense: the creaking door. We end with the terrified narrator overcome with "helplessness".

Finding a structure:

I had a lot of responses and wasn't sure how to organize them. Would I be able to include them all? When I read the questions I felt I didn't want to structure my essay in that order, though I wanted to discuss especially points 1, 3 and 4. I decided to go back more or less to my original idea and structure it around: Frankenstein's dilemma; the fiend; and the setting.

Sample essay on *Frankenstein* passage

This passage from Mary Shelley's <u>Frankenstein</u> *focuses on the terrifying decision that Frankenstein has to make as he nears the completion of his second being, a female fiend designed to be a companion to his first creation. The night setting and the sudden appearance of the fiend at this crucial moment create both suspense and terror as we experience the situation through the thoughts and feelings of the narrator.*

Frankenstein has experienced the effects of his first creation, "whose unparalleled barbarity had desolated my heart and filled it for ever with the bitterest remorse", but has been persuaded and threatened by the fiend into making a companion for him. He is now torn between this promise and the possible, imagined consequences of such an act, made worse because of the uncertainty. She could be 'ten thousand times more malignant than her mate" – the hyperbole stresses the horror of the idea. She might be repelled by the fiend, and exacerbate his situation. Worse, they might propagate a "race of devils" that might terrorize mankind. Frankenstein's train of thought culminates in a vital question that pits his own situation against the future of mankind. Can he for his own peace of existence risk the future of mankind? He has a kind of moral epiphany: "the wickedness of my promise (to the fiend) burst upon me", making him see the "selfishness" of protective action. This clarifies the ethics of the decision, but at this point Frankenstein's train of thought, in which we have been closely involved, is suspended by events: the fiend suddenly appears at the window to "claim the fulfilment" of the scientist's promise.

This is unexpected and frightening because we have been so closely following the thoughts of the narrator that the visual impact of this image is very strong. In addition, the order of the narration makes the horror greater. First, the narrator is in a heightened state of emotion from the realization of what he might be responsible for: "I trembled, and my heart failed within me". Then, he looks up by chance and sees "by the light of the moon, the daemon at the casement". The fact that he sees moonlight first, then the fiend framed against this, makes the image more eerie and sinister. The indistinctness of the monster, only described by the one detail of a "ghastly grin" wrinkling his lips, heightens the horror. The grin, so out of place, suggests his power over the Doctor, but Frankenstein also has power as he madly and fearfully tears to pieces his new creation, thwarting the hopes of the fiend. The diction with which the fiend is now described, the "malice and treachery" on his face, his howl of "revenge" build suspense as it suggests an evil from which there will be no escape.

After this dramatic action Shelley introduces an effective contrast between the emotionally devastated Frankenstein, his state made worse by being utterly alone with his "terrible reveries", and the peacefulness and harmony of the scene outside his apartment window. The diction and images –aural, visual and tactile –create a tranquil effect: the "almost motionless" sea, the "hushed" winds, the "quiet moon", the "gentle breeze". The fishermen calling to one another are a reminder of a simple supportive community, contrasting with the isolation and harmful sophistication of the solitary scientist. The "profound" silence and the peace of the scene lulls us, so that the sudden introduction of a strange sound ("the paddling of oars", the landing of a person close to the house) creates suspense and fear.

The last paragraph focuses on the terror of the narrator, trembling and helpless as his private space is once again menaced, so overcome he is unable to seek assistance. That he is unable to name the horror, but feels a "presentiment of who it was", makes the menace seem greater, as does the appeal to the sense of sound alone, the creaking of the door, the attempt " to open it softly".

In this vivid passage Shelley powerfully suggests mental, emotional and physical horror, through the description of feelings, the force of diction, the setting and the building of suspense. By taking us so deeply into the mind and senses of Frankenstein, she effectively makes us share the narrator's terrifying experience.

Student evaluation of the essay

I felt that I had been able to include everything I wanted to say, and I was pleased that I was able to comment quite a bit on features. I realized halfway through that I seemed to be structuring the commentary in a linear way, even though I'd planned it in three sections following my three ideas. However, it was easier to write because I know what I was focusing on, and I think this helps hold it together. I also realized that I had more or less followed the topics in the guiding questions. However, I think that my essay was better, more inspired and more detailed, because I started with my own responses, than if I had simply worked out answers to the questions.

6. Some reminders for the exam room

- *Take time to read and plan carefully.* You should aim to read the text at least three times. Your reading and planning may take up to half an hour (perhaps a little more for Higher). DO NOT begin to write before your plan is clear. Remember that if you read and respond with care, you are more likely to have understood the text appropriately, and the writing will flow fairly easily as a result. This is a test of how well you think and respond, not how much you write. Look back at the models for planning in "The Black Lace Fan" and *Frankenstein* examples above, which identify both significant features and details. Pay particular attention to the *effects* of language and features, as you think out your response. This is where many candidates lose marks.

- *Read the title, and any details supplied at the end of the passage, attentively.* The title, date and endnotes may provide you with important clues as to content and how you should read the passage. (For example, *The Horse's Mouth* prose passage above supplies important information about the narrator.)

- *Avoid a rigid formula as a strategy.* Each poem or passage will have its own particular features.

- *Don't try to reduce the passage or poem to a single 'message' or meaning.* The prose will probably be part of a longer work, so 'message' is inappropriate anyway. With a poem, be alert to ambiguities and complexities of effect, to the suggestiveness of the work. This is a more appropriate approach than trying to reduce it to a 'message'.

- *Don't use the passage or poem as a springboard for your own opinions or experiences.* Your task is to respond to the content of the passage or poem itself and how effectively it is constructed and expressed. Your feelings and opinions, for example about Frankenstein's creation, are not what is required.

- *Do not make detailed references to other works,* for the same reason as the above item. A passing reference that illuminates the meaning of the text may be acceptable.

- *You don't have to praise the passage.* It is selected because there are interesting things to be said about it; it may not be a 'great' work. Avoid insincerity.

- *Avoid the mere identification of literary features or technical devices.* You should be able to identify features, but in order to discuss how they create or underline meaning and effect.

- *Support ideas and statements with close reference to the text.* Lengthy quotations, however, are unnecessary.

- *Don't simply avoid the difficult bits.* Honest doubts and the addressing of ambiguities are acceptable.

- *Do write enough for this to be a developed piece of work*, for example, four to five sides. If you have planned carefully, observing the models, 'having enough to say' should not be too much of a problem.

- *Do proofread your work carefully*, punctuating it intelligently and eliminating colloquialism and grammatical errors. You will lose marks for carelessness.

A Bibliography for Commentary

You will probably not have the time to work through more than one or two of the following books, so only the texts most specific to this task (all of them written addressing the student) have been selected. Remember to address both prose and poetry

David Lodge, The Art of Fiction, Secker and Warburg, 1992
This provides fifty different short prose passages from a wide variety of novels, each illustrating a different literary term or concept (such as symbolism, repetition, suspense, etc.) Each is accompanied by a clear discussion of the selected literary feature. Informative, stimulating and accessible, it introduces you to many different kinds of prose as well as features, and is good for the exam essay (novel) as well as commentary.

Malcolm Peet and David Robinson, Leading Questions, Nelson, 1992
Written for students taking British unseen commentary exams, this is a detailed and stimulating self-help course that will teach you a lot about reading prose and poetry closely and critically. Questions and exercises help you tackle a wide range of passages and poems for understanding in depth.

Laurence Perrine, Sound and Sense: *An Introduction to Poetry, Harcourt Brace, Revised 1992*
One of the most thorough and helpful introductions to poetry, and a 'classic'. It helps you focus on different aspects such as figurative language, tone, rhythm, metre,and musical devices, by selecting a number of poems that illustrate those features. Discussions of each feature and of many of the poems are provided.

Don Shiach, The Critical Eye: Appreciating prose and poetry, Nelson, 1989
Prepared for students taking British unseen commentary exams, it offers a wide and interesting choice of prose passages and poetry, accompanied by analysis and questions to help you appreciate important features and techniques.

H.S.Toshack, Writing Unseen Commentaries: A Student Help Book, 2002, (available from the website http://www.litworks.com)
This is specifically written for I.B. H and S Level students. It takes a number of passages from past I.B. papers and other sources to illustrate different aspects such as setting, character, and action, and provides analysis of further passages.

Jeffrey and Lynn Wood, Cambridge Critical Workshop, Cambridge 1995
Written by teachers for students doing British unseen commentary exams, this is also useful for I.B. students. It introduces you to many styles and periods of prose and poetry though a wide selection of passages, and provides guidelines for approaching each of them, as well as some general guidelines for commentary. There are also sample student essays to demonstrate appropriate responses.

1. Introduction

The need for independent strategies

The study of your texts is the basis of your programme. How well you do this and what kinds of strategies you employ in studying determines the quality of your performance in these three assessed areas. There are many texts to cover in the 18 months of the programme (15 texts at Higher Level, 11 at Standard) and there is rarely time in the school year to study them all in the depth the teacher might ideally wish to, or the depth you'll need for good results. In addition, there is not always time for teacher-led revision. So you will need to develop some personal strategies for your independent study and revision.

The genres covered here

The suggestions in this chapter are intended to serve for the study of all your texts, though there will be an emphasis on preparation for the examination essay. Although the hope is that you will put these strategies into practice from the beginning of the course, they should successfully serve as revision (re-reading) guidelines. The focus will be on drama and the novel, as these are two of the most common genres studied for A1. There are more revision strategies for both prose and poetry in Chapter One: The Exam Commentary, and for all genres in Chapter Three: The Examination Essay. You should read these in conjunction with this chapter.

Non-fiction and the short story overlap to some extent with novels, and the strategies described here will help with them, along with a section on non-fiction in Chapter Four: The Oral Component. Texts referred to will be some of those most commonly studied.

Avoiding common weaknesses

One aim of this chapter is to help you study in such a way that common weaknesses should not mar your work. These include:

- 'telling the story' of texts rather than being analytical
- not discussing the texts in depth and detail
- not understanding the 'literary features' of these genres

If you follow the steps and attempt the questions below, you should find yourself approaching the texts in an analytical way, the essential basis for answering the question appropriately. The questions are designed to make you think!

2. Studying plays

Should I read the whole play first, before I try to make sense of it in detail?

There is an advantage to this, because you need to get a feel for the whole. It can be satisfying, as in reading a novel or story, to find out what happens. By reading it straight through you can establish some essentials early on in your study: the line of action, the focus of interest, the situation of the central character(s), and the kind of world the play projects. You will then be more attentive to how the details of the scenes contribute to these, when you begin your second reading, which should involve some careful notes. Some students, however, like to plunge straight in, noting details from the start, finding a focus to each act or scene as they go, and tying it together at the end.

Whichever way you do it, you need to work through the following aspects. As you work through each step in relation to your own texts, remember that many exam questions have been based on these very aspects.

How much background to drama should I know?

As you begin each play, you should be aware of the period the authors were writing in and the theatrical conventions of those times. You should know broadly (where these are relevant) the traditions of Greek Theatre, of Shakespeare's age, of late 19th century Europe, and mid to late 20th century Europe and America, as most commonly studied plays come from these four eras. Many of your playwrights were highly individual and experimental in their writing, so you also need to know what they contributed to the development of drama, and the influences upon them. The bibliography at the end of this chapter suggests some resources.

Finding a focus to the play on a first reading

(a) Action or 'plot' versus 'story'

It is important to see the clear-cut lines or shape of the plot or action, of what *happens* in the play. 'Plot' suggests a sequence of actions or events organized in such a way as to suggest a logic of development from a beginning to an end that seems inevitable. You should be able to describe this in no more than one or two sentences. Plot is very dominant and intricate in some plays, but less so in others where psychological interest in characters may be more significant, as in *A Streetcar Named Desire*.

Yet something does happen in *Streetcar*; there *is* a development of action. So we could say that the plot line is:

Blanche arrives seeking refuge from a troubled past at her married sister's apartment in New Orleans, but antagonizes Stella's husband Stan by her behaviour. He thwarts her romantic hopes, and in different ways (including rape) overpowers her to the point where her fragile mental world collapses and she is taken to an insane asylum.

Six verbs in these two sentences sum up the main action line (though verbs like "antagonizes" and "overpowers" cover several kinds of action).

We can now distinguish this from the whole 'story' of Blanche, which emerges in fragments at intervals through the dialogue but not chronologically. This concerns:

her aristocratic Southern upbringing, her disastrous early marriage, her struggle to support her ailing, decadent family, and her escape into prostitution. Prostitution and an affair with a student ruin her reputation and career and bring her to the precarious state we see her in at the start of the play, jeopardising her chances of a new start.

Although this is an interesting 'story', we can see by comparing the two how the playwright Tennessee Williams makes a memorable *play* by choosing to begin it halfway through the 'story', and focusing on the struggle between the three central characters, especially Blanche and Stan, and the 'cause and effect' of their relationship. The gradual revelation of selected details of her *story*, during the play, and the part these play in the action, the way they affect other characters, is an important part of the interest.

Now try doing this for your play texts, distinguishing story from plot or action in one or two sentences. Answering exam questions often necessitates holding the whole plot or sequence in your head (without getting bogged down in details) so that you can select the important moments to illustrate your answer. Make a plan of the action. What is interesting about the construction of the plot? What is significant about the way bits of the story are revealed or introduced?

(b) The central character's predicament and its ramifications

Although there may be some exceptions, this is at the heart of most plays. You need to identify it clearly and see the part it plays in the shape and meaning of the play, and how that predicament provokes further problems or complications. In some cases there may be a dual predicament where there are two more or less equally important central characters, such as Creon and Antigone in Sophocles' *Antigone*.

One might say that Antigone's predicament is not that she must choose between family and state obligations (her mind is already made up), but that the price she must pay for burying her brother is death. This implicates all those near to her, in different ways, especially as most of them feel it is wrong for her to be punished. Similarly one could say that Creon's predicament is that, having made a decision in the interests of a strong and stable state, he finds himself opposed on all sides including by those dearest to him like his son.

Blanche's predicament is that she desperately needs security, but her guilt about her previous life, her lies to conceal it, and the deceptive façade she presents, make such security impossible. The pattern of events, and the outcome of the 'predicament' are central to the meaning of each text, deliberately chosen and crafted for the effect they produce.

What is that effect, in these, or other texts you have read? Make a diagram or spidergram of the predicament and what that leads to in terms of conflict and action.

c) Conflict and tension between characters

This is one of the most fascinating aspects of a play and is something you should identify on your first reading, by making a diagram of the different lines of conflict or tension between characters. What kinds of conflict do you see, and what do they lead to? How many of the characters are involved?

In the case of *Streetcar*, we might see the diagram as a triangle. The basic tension line is a struggle between Blanche and Stan both for territory and for Stella. Considering the strength of the Stella / Stan relationship and their domestic life, this would be a hard one for Blanche to win. But the outcome is not so simple. There is the strong bond of background and family between the sisters. Stella may choose Stan over Blanche at a crucial moment, but seeing him responsible for Blanche's breakdown isn't easily acceptable to her.

The play thus ends on a note of ambiguity, indicating the complexity of family relationships and bonds. We might say that Stella does not so much show tension herself, as exist at the centre of it, making the battle between the more deadly rivals more acute.

In other plays, the tension lines may be more varied, spread between more characters, but the basic lines leading to the outcome should be clear. In *Hedda Gabler* three men have different relationships with Hedda (her husband, their friend Brack, and her ex-lover Lovberg). Only Brack is prepared to fight for his territory by destroying the ex-lover, and consequently Hedda (this is the outcome). Neither the husband nor Lovberg realize there is such a contest.

Parallel to this, Hedda fights for her ex-lover Lovberg by destroying his new relationship with Thea, who is unaware of the deadliness of the contest. So lines of tension may be one-way, not mutual, creating a subtlety and irony of effect.

Look for the tension in terms of the action and outcome in your plays. Look too, for the source(s) of conflict. Is it on a point of principle and morality, as in *Antigone*? Is it sexual, social, territorial, a mixture of these or something else?

(d) The world the characters inhabit; worlds in contrast or tension

We often say how in each of Shakespeare's tragedies he creates a distinct 'world': of the claustrophobic, untrustworthy court in *Hamlet*, of night and terror in *Macbeth*, of storm and heath in *King Lear*. Images, values, objects, references, relationships – all play a part in creating this world.

In *Death of a Salesman*, football, trophies, cars, refrigerators, tape-recorders, offices, houses, and many other objects and aspects of setting, add up to a material world where the dream of and struggle for material success is central, and such success is the consuming value. The family world mirrors the wider society driven by the American Dream, and is distorted by it. As in many plays, another, contrasting world is glimpsed: a simpler, rural, freer environment (of Willy's past, and Biff's Texas), where life and beauty can be savoured, counter-pointing the material urban world that is engulfing and destroying this family.

In *Streetcar* the predominant world is the easy-going, bustling, racially and socially mixed environment of New Orleans, the 'new' industrial American society. It is a world of poker games, bowling, eating, drinking, jazz, bars, camaraderie. Set against this is another, partly fantasy world (Blanche's), of fine clothes, art, literature, classical music, baths, beaux, money: a 'cultivated' world of 'intelligence and breeding' as in the myth of the Old South. The uneasy contrast and clash between these two worlds, each with something to recommend them, is at the heart of the play's conflicts.

What are some of the dominant images, objects, settings, relationships, and attitudes in each of your texts? What kind of a picture or world does it add up to? You will find that whereas in some plays like *Streetcar* and *Death of a Salesman* concrete objects are plentiful and significant, in others, like *The Crucible* they are very rare, and it is *attitudes* that create the picture. How might you define this picture in a few adjectives? Is a critical attitude towards it implied, as in *Death of a Salesman,* or a sympathetic one? Are two worlds juxtaposed? Plays are more than characters in a setting. They are closely related to their societies, and the author's view of these societies is essential to our understanding of the plays.

Having established broad outlines and central issues in your texts, you should now consider some of the most important features in drama.

Characters

This is a major topic, and frequently emerges in exam questions. We will focus on four important aspects: presentation, change, complexity of relationships, and relation to issues

(a) Methods of presentation

> First, think of your own play texts. How are different characters made known to you? You should rapidly be able to think of at least three ways.
>
> 1.
>
> 2.
>
> 3

For example:

- There may be detailed stage instructions as in G.B. Shaw, Miller, Williams and others, where qualities of character, appearance, clothes, may be specified in some detail.

- Main characters may be described by others before we meet them, though this may not be completely reliable or the character may change (Hedda Gabler, Macbeth).

- There may be no introduction; instead, the character appears and speaks, revealing him/herself in the process (Antigone, King Lear). Monologue or soliloquy are conventions permitting quite detailed self-revelation, in addition to dialogue.

- How the character speaks and behaves in relation to a spectrum of characters may be revealing of different aspects of a complex personality (Hedda, Nora)

- The speech patterns or habits characters use, or their language and references, may characterize them (Blanche's poetic symbolism, Stan's references to poker).

- Gestures and actions may indicate a lot. John Proctor in Arthur Miller's *The Crucible* salts the dinner while his wife is out of the room, then comments to her that it is 'well-seasoned'. This indicates something of his sensual nature and needs, his difference from his wife, and his desire to placate her. Blanche's drinking of the whisky when alone, signals the state of her nerves, her alcoholism and her deception.

How many of these overlap with your ideas? Have you found some others? In any one text, how many different kinds of presentation can you find for any one character, or contrasting kinds for several characters?

Blanche is characterized partly by dress, but different colour dresses underline different aspects of her (the fluffy white dress, the red kimono and bra, the 'Della Robbia' blue outfit). She is also characterised by what she says, but again, this varies according to the person she is speaking to and the impression she may want to create. Her actions (for example drinking, bathing, smoking), also say much about her. All the other main characters make statements about her, but is any one of them 'right', as far as we see the picture?

Why do you think an author has chosen any one of these methods in a particular instance? For example, Hedda's aunt-in-law and the maid discuss her before she appears, sending conflicting messages but indicating some unease about her character, which is quickly borne out, foreshadowing conflicts and suggesting social differences. Lear, on the other hand, takes us all by surprise at the beginning of the play by making the decisions that he does, thus linking us closely with the reactions of the characters.

To understand the craft of building complex characters clearly, it can be helpful to make a chart. In the left hand column you list facts, ideas and impressions about a character. In the next column, facing these, you indicate where you derived them (inferences from an action or words of the character; someone else's words, stage directions, etc.).

Remember that different time periods and theatrical conventions affect the manner of presentation. Appearance and subtle differences in tone of voice is irrelevant to Greek theatre where actors wore masks and often doubled, playing different parts, and where only men performed. How far do such conventions affect the presentation of characters you might consider? What time periods and different conventions do your plays come from?

(b) Evolving or static characters

Consider two or three of your characters at the beginning and end of the plays they are in. Have they changed? Have they learnt something? If so, what has brought about this change and/or learning?

Character 1.
Character 2.

Now consider the following and jot down some responses:

- Is the change positive or negative?

- Was it brought about by force of circumstance and reflection, through the need to make a choice or decision, through the influence of another's words, or some other agent? What changes Biff, for example, in *Death of a Salesman*? What makes John Proctor decide to accept death?

- Were the characters self-deceived and did that change into self-discovery? Was this liberating or agonizing? If so, at what point? Or are there a series of discoveries?

- Which characters remain static? Is this necessarily negative? Kent and Cordelia in *King Lear* represent, among other things, the reassuring constancy of love and loyalty. It is important and moving that their natures do *not* change.

- Why do you think the author might have chosen to make the character change or remain the same? What effect is produced by this?

34

Take one or two cases of a changed character and of a static character and suggest why the author has made this choice. What impact does it have on us? What, if anything, has Linda or Happy learnt by the end of *Death of a Salesman*?

Look carefully at the moments of change, the speeches or dialogue relating to the change. These will be key moments in the play.

(c) The complexity of characters and relationships

As in life, characters may have a mixture of feelings, attitudes and motives towards others. The kind of 'realistic' plays that reflect this complexity are fascinating because of this. We might say that Blanche is attracted by Stan on a sexual level (he is a 'man') but also repelled by his violence and primitive nature (he is an 'ape') and his lack of social and educational background. She fears him because her security depends on him, and he is antagonistic towards her, because she threatens his domestic stability, is 'false', and so on.

Draw a line between two of the central characters in one of your plays. Along the line place an arrow running from Blanche to Stan, for example, and write along this her feelings for him. Now add a parallel arrow from Stan to Blanche, and write along that the main feelings he has for her. You will see how different these feelings are, and that accounts for the complexity of tension and conflict. Add arrows from each of them to Stella and back, and you will begin to see at a glance how complex the core of relationships is at the heart of this play.

(d) The characters' connection to issues, themes and values

Characters are part of a complex web of meaning in plays. If you make a concise chart of the philosophy, values, or ideas held by each character, and see how each connects or conflicts with those of other characters, you will begin to appreciate this web. Meaning may be developed through parallels and contrasts or through grouping characters. In *Death of a Salesman*, a number of characters (Willy, Charley, Bernard, and Howard among them) are 'office' men, but behave differently. Charley and Bernard are successful, but also honest, kind and generous, unaffected by 'image'. Howard is successful, but ruthless; Willy is a failure in business terms, but needs to dream that he is successful. Values are at the heart of this play and it is important to see how they are established.

Another way to explore the presentation of values (and this may also show the complexity of characters) is to take a central value, such as 'honesty' in *Hamlet*, and create a scale of 0-10 on which you try to place some of the main characters, with references to parts of the play that justify your choice. How honest are the old school friends Rosencrantz and Guildenstern, 0 or a 2, or more? At least they admit they 'were sent for'. How honest is Hamlet?

A central character may hold views or behave in ways opposite to those the playwright wants to support (though he or she may remain sympathetic, like Willy in *Salesman*). Or s/he may embody the playwright's ideas or beliefs, like Sophocles' Antigone, respecting the Gods, and family obligations. On the other hand the 'meaning' may be ambiguous or ambivalent. For example, characters representing opposite viewpoints and values may each contain something worthwhile, such as the aristocrats on the one hand, and the rising bourgeois characters on the other, in Chekhov's *The Cherry Orchard*. Are any of these three approaches relevant to your plays?

What values or issues are at the heart of your plays? How are these made known to you? Through a key speech, through the outcome of characters' fates in the play, or in some other way?

Structure

There is no one structure that is 'right' or typical of plays, though at different times in theatrical history certain structures have became popular. Each play has its own particular structure (or order and pattern of events) and this has to do with the best way to tell that particular story. There is considerable variety of structure.

Streetcar is divided into eleven scenes which track a fairly concentrated sequence of events or episodes over several months, concerning Blanche and her stay in her sister's apartment and the fateful movement towards disaster. Each scene has a dramatic logic of its own; it focuses in detail on one situation or event that is developed and in some way resolved. This permits a complex revelation of character and relationship. Placed side by side, the scenes show patterns, parallels and repetitions that give the play a poetic density and meaning as well as indicating development.

For example, Scene Three is a "Poker Night", with tension between the men playing in the kitchen, and the women in the bedroom. A relationship begins to form between Blanche and Mitch. The final Scene Eleven is also a poker night, identical in some respects, again with the worlds of men and women separated, but it is also the moment of Blanche's removal to the sanatorium, Mitch is broken by it all, and Stella torn in her loyalties. The similarities sharpen the differences and are a measure of what has evolved.

In contrast, Sophocles' *Antigone* (like other Greek tragedies) forms one continuous structure, showing the rapid development of action over one day. This allows a sharp focus on the tragic developments stemming from a single decision and a sense of the horrifying inevitability of the outcome. *Death of a Salesman* divides into two acts that interweave complex revelations of past and present, but focus on Biff's return home and his futile attempt to achieve his father's dream for him. Other plays may be divided into three or four acts that have a more 'classic' structure of exposition, complication, climax and resolution, aspects that allow the author to pace, develop and organize the plot effectively.

- How are your plays structured, and why do you think the authors have made these choices in relation to their material?

- What patterns or repetitions can you see in the way they are put together?

- Is there a pattern to the opening and closing of the play and if so, what is suggested by this? Ibsen's *A Doll's House* begins with Nora happily entering the house, and ends with her resolutely leaving it.

- Look at the different sections of your plays, whether acts or scenes or (as in Greek plays) episodes. What is the focus of each of them? How do they relate to each other? What is the cumulative effect? How is interest maintained? What are the key points – of crisis or revelation, for example – and how are these brought about?

Language and Style

These are often confused. Language is the method of communication, using words that may involve poetry and song as well as dialogue. Gesture and action also count as language, as communication. Some plays have been entirely or partly wordless. Thus we may say that the language of *Lear,* the method of communication in that play, involves riddles and song (which emphasise ideas) as well as the prose and poetry of the dialogue. Similarly *Streetcar* uses songs that are both lyrics of the era but also comment figuratively or symbolically on Blanche's situation, aligning her with more universal situations.

Different characters in the same play may use language in very different ways. Sentence length and complexity, the kind of grammar and diction used, the field of reference or allusion, and the tone and manner suggested by the speech can play a part in characterization and establishing differences between characters. Stanley's sentences in *Streetcar* are short, colloquial, and characterized by diction drawn from card-playing and bets. This isn't just realistic, the kind of language such a man would use, but makes a point about his outlook on life: aggressive, individualistic and competitive, tough on losers.

Blanche's language fits with her elevated Southern background and her former profession as an English teacher, with references to Edgar Allen Poe and other writers, and to artists like

Della Robbia. To that extent it is 'naturalistic'. But she also often uses language symbolically, referring for example to the 'searchlight' that was switched off her world at her husband's death, or candles glowing in the baby's life. This emphasizes her emotional depth and the sense of tragedy in her life.

Style is the writer's distinctive manner of writing or speaking. We might say for example that Pinter's style is characterized by gaps, silences, non-sequitors, and fragments, or Chekhov's by apparent inconclusiveness. See the glossary for a further definition of style.

Take two or more of your plays and select two or three characters from each play. Look at a section of dialogue involving each of these characters and note what characterizes their language in each case, and how that affects both the way we see them, and the effect of the play as a whole.

3. Studying Novels

Unlike plays, which are usually clearly structured and comparatively short, novels are often long and may seem diffuse and complex. How can they be made manageable and coherent through study? Even teachers can find that task hard, though many have devised successful ways to do it. The following suggestions assume you are studying independently, revising, or need to add to class work.

Will one reading suffice?

Ideally, read it once for the pleasure of immersing yourself and finding out what happens, then a second time (for example with the class) focusing on the artistry and details. A short novel you can re-read at the revision stage, but a long one such as *Anna Karenina* you may only have time to read once, so the strategy such as the following is important. This also works as a revision strategy.

How to take effective notes

(i) Focusing in detail on selected passages

One way to establish coherence is to select a series of passages of 40-50 lines (a page to a page and a half) for close reading and analysis as you go through the work, for example every fifty or hundred pages, depending on the length and density of the work. This works very well for the detailed study of Part Two texts in preparation for the 'Formal Oral', and for all 'classical' texts.

Begin with the opening page, which should provide clues about how the novel is to be read, and its distinctive features. For example, take the opening of *Pride and Prejudice*. Read the following passage and decide (noting in the margin) what you think are its 'distinctive features'. These may concern content, style, and point of view. It is helpful to look for any tensions, contrasts or 'oppositions', amongst other elements. It is these that create interest, as you will see below. You should also note what you don't understand, or what you feel you may need to know more about.

Sample analysis of the opening page of *Pride and Prejudice* by Jane Austen

It is a truth universally acknowledged, that a single man in possession of a good fortune must be in want of a wife. However little known the feelings or views of such a man may be on his first entering the neighbourhood, this truth is so well fixed in the minds of the surrounding families that he is considered as the rightful property of some one or another of their daughters.
"My dear Mr. Bennet", said his lady to him one day, "have you heard that Netherfield Park is to be let at last?"
Mr. Bennet replied that he had not.
"But it is", returned she; "for Mrs Long has just been here, and she told me all about it".
Mr. Bennet made no answer.
"Do you not want to know who has taken it?" cried his wife impatiently.
"*You* want to tell me, and I have no objection to hearing it".
This was invitation enough.

> "Why, my dear, you must know, Mrs Long says that Netherfield is taken by a young man of large fortune from the north of England; that he came down on Monday in a chaise and four to see the place, and was so much delighted with it that he agreed with Mr. Morris immediately; that he is to take possession before Michaelmas, and some of his servants are to be in the house by the end of next week."
>
> "What is his name?"
>
> "Bingley".
>
> "Is he married, or single?"
>
> "Oh, single, my dear, to be sure! A single man of large fortune; four or five thousand a year. What a fine thing for our girls!"
>
> "How so? How can it affect them?"
>
> "My dear Mr Bennet", replied his wife, "how can you be so tiresome! You must know, of course, that I am thinking of his marrying one of them".
>
> "Is that his design in settling here?"
>
> "Design! Nonsense, how can you talk so! But it is very likely that he may fall in love with one of them, and therefore you must visit him as soon as he comes".

Your main responses might be to:

(a) The centrality of *dialogue*. We are plunged into this without introduction to the couple, but it provides:

- details of the dramatic new situation (the arrival of the wealthy single stranger in the neighbourhood)
- characterization of the couple through the rhythms of their respective speeches and the differences in their reaction to the news
- a certain comedy of effect stemming from the author's manipulation of their differences
- dramatic effectiveness and immediacy, as we seem to be witnessing a conversation take place; the dialogue is not broken up with 'stage directions' or authorial comments

(b) *The theme*: the transparency of interest in marriage (connected with 'fortune', a word repeated three times), and the predatory, competitive nature of the mothers of the community in this respect

(c) The *position* and (ironic) *attitude* of the narrator. Her sweeping pronouncement opens the book, but it may take a second reading to see that the 'universal' truth about the needs of single rich men is an ironic comment on the mentality of a small community. More specifically it satirizes the mothers in such a community who surely do not recognize that they consider such a man the 'rightful property of some one or another of their daughters'.

(d) *Tension* between:

- the formality of tone and language, and the implicit mockery of the behaviour described
- the author's understanding of her subjects, and their limited understanding of themselves
- the Bennets' respective intentions and attitudes. Each sees the situation differently. We seem to be invited to read this with some critical awareness, with a little distance.

As you go further in your study of literary features (outlined below in this chapter) identification and discussion of authorial voice, dialogue, and so on, will become easier. Response to content and to artistry will begin to merge and you will be able to understand that these are indivisible: narrative strategies create meaning and effect.

If you were to continue reading *Pride and Prejudice* using this method of selecting passages and analysing them attentively, each one would lead on to a deeper appreciation of the distinctiveness and complexity of the work (content and features). It would sharpen your awareness of the issues here: the role of parents, the standpoint of the narrator, marriage as a personal, social, and economic issue, and so on. In addition you would see the relation of one part to another more clearly.

(ii) Creating order in chapters or sections using headings and key points

This method helps you keep control over your reading as you go along, to keep plot lines clear. It makes it easier to connect ideas, to review sections and, eventually, the whole book. Allow space to add in ideas from class and your re-reading later. For each chapter:

- Create a heading or title, or a sentence summarizing the main action
- Bullet point a series of significant aspects, indicating your responses briefly. The aspects might be to do with content, or narrative strategies, or both. For example:

Sample of chapter notes organized in headings:

Great Expectations: Chapter Two: "_The forge and the theft_"

Introduction to the forge, Joe and Mrs Joe: striking characterization using various methods:
significance of clothing (apron- symbolic overtones);
accessories ('tickler');
idiosyncrasies and repetitions of speech ("Ram-page", "by hand")
narrator's summary of qualities and physical description;
significant action (the bread-cutting); vivid similes cutting bread "as If she were making a plaister".
Reversal of usual man/wife roles or characteristics. Funny or serious, or both?

The comic relationship of Pip and Joe. I learnt in class this was Dickens' starting point for the novel. Extended comic mime sequence of bread and butter eating and later, bread concealing. Visual and dramatic. But relationship also serious –the most significant in Pip's life

Discussion of convicts and Hulks. Pip's questioning. Bright child. Sense of authorities (army, law, etc) versus wretched individual.

Pip's conscience about theft; he identifies with criminals.

Details of the food Pip steals (each item takes on significance later). Food a powerful indicator of relationships and attitudes.

Notice how the title or caption pulls the plot and novel development together. Note too that you can extend such jottings later. The forge, Pip and Joe, the convict, Pip's conscience, food, are all to assume great significance as the novel goes on.

(iii) Pulling several chapters together: finding patterns and connections

At the end of a section (this might be five chapters, for example) review the points made already from your reading and see what patterns or groupings of characters and issues you can find. This makes the mass of detail more coherent and manageable.

Sample of patterns and connections found In the first five chapters of Great Expectations

- Two contrasting settings. the lonely and dismal marshes, and the forge, where there is fire, love, food (though also harshness). Pip connects these two, taking food from forge to starving convict.

- Connection as well as distinction between Pip and convict?

- Pip - victim of adult demands and violence – with convict and Mrs Joe producing sense of guilt.

After another five or ten more chapters, look for patterns between the first and second units of reading:

- Story so far based on _two_ extraordinary and random encounters (convict and Miss H) that engage Pip against his will and give him a secret inner experience that also isolates him from others. Pip has a certain (compassionate) relationship with both these.

- Three women of different ages and types (Mrs Joe, Miss H, Estella) – all treat Pip badly.

- Different groups of values in characters emerging: the _hypocritical and mercenary_ (Mrs J. Pumblechook, Miss H's 'toady' relatives); and the _compassionate and sensitive_ (Joe, Pip). Miss H in a category of her own at the moment. The values, interestingly, cross class boundaries.

- Another contrasting pair of settings: forge and Satis House –now seen as _class_ divide for Pip. This gives rise to shame – a new feeling for Pip.

(iv) Journal entries

Some of the weaknesses in performance in all assessed components in A1 are lack of depth, perceptiveness and an independent critical approach. Research has shown that the use of journals or free writing on selected parts of the work helps develop these qualities. Some teachers use this method, but it is also an alternative to the methods of note taking described above. You can mix these methods in your study. Some students use the word processor successfully to record their responses rapidly and freely, as in the following example.

Sample of a student journal entry

This journal entry was on an individually chosen chapter of the first twelve chapters of *Great Expectations*. Students were asked to write freely on a passage or chapter they had particularly enjoyed and/or found interesting. The assignment was not an essay and structure was not emphasized. Development of ideas was the priority.

I found Chapter 9 the most enjoyable and interesting chapter so far for a number of reasons. After the hugely complex, mysterious and transforming experience of Chapter 8 (Satis House) this was like comic relief, but I also found it psychologically interesting - Pip's behaviour and my response.

Pip gives reasons for lying (I'm not sure this is the most appropriate word even though they use it) about what happened to him at Miss Havisham's, but are they the real ones? He says he had a "dread of not being understood", and that "there would be something coarse and treacherous" about describing Miss H. as she really was, to Mrs Joe. To me these reasons are very different. Pip has experienced something overwhelmingly personal and life-changing at Satis House. In a way he has been given a privileged glimpse into a style of life that Mr Pumblechook and Mrs Joe have been excluded from. Miss H has in a way made him a kind of confidant and he has understood something about her feelings. He has been entranced by Estella but through her has also realized something shattering about himself – that he's 'coarse and common'. But even realizing that puts him above the forge. So here is something of his own, for once, and I can understand why he can't share it. It's too complex and it's too personal, and it also puts him in a different category from the adults round him.

It's true that they wouldn't understand this experience, and might think he was lying and so punish him, but for me another important thing is that for once he's in control, he has power over these two horrible adults who have always bullied and mistreated and despised him, and can give rein to his imagination, which must give him a great sense of release. As he says, he was 'reckless'. What he tells them is more like a fairy story, more fanciful than the tragic and psychologically twisted 'reality' of Satis House. Perhaps this is more what he would like to have seen:
' " She was sitting", I answered, in a black velvet coach".
Mr Pumblechook and Mrs Joe stared at one another –as they well might – and both repeated, "In a black velvet coach?".
"Yes", said I, "And Miss Estella –that's her niece, I think – handed her in cake and wine at the coach window, on a gold plate. And we all had cake and wine on gold plates" '.

This is like dramatic irony because we, the readers, know what happened and can enjoy the spectacle of them being fooled. Surely Dickens must have enjoyed making them look ridiculous. This also brings us into a different relationship with Pip, at least in this chapter, because in a way we become accomplices rather than witnesses or viewers of what happens to him. Having read *Pride and Prejudice* I thought it was interesting how both authors use this technique of one character telling another about an event that we have shared, but distorting it or telling it in a way that shows something about their character.

Joe takes these 'lies' very seriously (telling Pip to pray about it, etc.) and I respect his point, but it's hard to see things the way he does. Dickens has made this difficult for us. We can't help enjoying it (and surely he did too), so are we really expected to judge the incident in such a moralistic way?

(I enjoyed writing this and I took about 30 minutes without stopping)

Comment on the sample

Take a moment to reflect on what this student has achieved, probably without knowing it. She has entered into the life of the narration, enjoying watching Pip, who is usually the victim, usually prevented from voicing his thoughts, become the storyteller, the one in charge. She has appreciated various literary features, and described their effects (dramatic irony, for example) in detail. She has also experimentally developed ideas that she may later want to adjust or confirm in the light of more reading.

Most interestingly, she has both challenged what seem to be the assumptions of the narration (that it was morally wrong to tell the 'lies') and in the last sentences opened up a possible contradiction in Dickens' approach. These last two aspects: the challenging of assumptions and the recognition of ambivalence or contradiction are significant ways in which traditional texts have come to be read.

Whether or not your teacher sets this kind of exercise, writing paragraphs of this kind, interspersed with the more structured kind of notes, will help you develop confidence in questioning, exploring and articulating ideas. Try two or three at least, in the course of reading a text.

4. Understanding and appreciating literary features in the novel

(i) Beginnings

These are very important. Novelists often labour over their beginnings to get them right. As with plays, beginnings introduce us to the new, unfamiliar and unique world of a particular work. Where is it set? Who is telling this story and why? How does the author or narrator want us to respond to it? Are there challenges of language and style? If we take time to assimilate the novel's many different aspects, and understand the territory, we can move smoothly on.

They also need to draw us in quickly. Think about two or three openings of novels you have read. How would you describe the strategies? Why do they work? Do they intentionally mislead us? (You can think about your plays in a similar way.) Do they:

*   Start in the *middle* of an action, conversation, or story?
*   Begin at the end (like Martin Amis's *Time's Arrow*)?
*   Feature an unusual narrator introducing him/herself in an unusual way (Huckleberry Finn)?
*   Describe a landscape or place or character?
*   Open with a philosophical or epigrammatic statement (*Anna Karenina*) or an ironic one (*Pride and Prejudice*)?
*   Introduce a 'frame' story or narrator (*Heart of Darkness*)?
*   Startle us with a unique style of writing?

(ii) Narrators

Drama 'shows', through the action on stage. Novels 'tell', and must have a teller. Effects in drama, such as sound, may be 'outside' the dialogue, and there is a certain freedom for the director about costume and setting for example. But in the novel absolutely everything is filtered through a narrator and is thus more highly controlled. This is the biggest difference between the genres when you are thinking about 'features'.

The choice of narrator and point of view has been described as the single most important choice the writer makes, because it is this that will affect the reader emotionally and morally as well as aesthetically. Some writers have changed the narrator in the course of the writing of the novel, and re-written it, because the effect was not right. Try changing the perspective of a novel you know and you will understand this. For example, change the first person Marlow in *Heart of Darkness*, to an omniscient narrator. Or change an omniscient narrator to the perspective of a particular character (the 'pear' incident from *Anna Karenina* described in Chapter Five: World Literature would illustrate this).

But the choice of narrator in a text does not mean just one kind exclusively. Sometimes a work will shift from one point of view or narrator to another within the work. For instance in

41

Kafka's *Metamorphosis* we sometimes see things through Gregor's eyes, but more typically see him omnisciently, from the outside. The dual effect is very powerful. We need to see him, *and* feel with him. Jean Rhys in *Wide Sargasso Sea* shifts between two main first-person narrators, each with a perspective on the other. Some novels have sections that are in first person and sections in third person.

(iii) 'First person' and 'omniscient' narrators

There is no complete agreement on the terms to define these concepts but *'first person'* (using the 'I') and *'third person'* or *'omniscient'* (which can seem 'impersonal' as in *Pride and Prejudice*) are commonly used. Within each of these categories there is a spectrum of possibilities. Both have been used throughout the three-hundred-year history of the novel.

The *'first person'* or 'I' narrator :

- May be the central character
- May be a character mainly telling the story of other characters (Nick in *The Great Gatsby*)
- May appear to confide in the reader, can present his/her thoughts and feelings but cannot present those of other characters from the inside
- May be 'unreliable' in that they have only limited knowledge of what they relate or have reason to be biased or have values we cannot share
- Has a particular advantage in sharing directly thoughts and feelings and impressions with the reader

The *third person or omniscient (all-knowing) narrator* is 'outside' the world of the novel and:

- May focus entirely on the tale itself and seem invisible
- Can enter into the consciousness of any character (as Tolstoy does with a number of characters in *Anna Karenina*)
- Can move in and out of a character, presenting both outside and inside (as in Kafka's *Metamorphosis*)
- Can use a variety of ways to present a character and his/her thoughts (description, dialogue, etc) as in Jane Austen's *Pride and Prejudice*.
- Can present a great range of characters

These lists are not comprehensive. They present a limited number of possibilities.
Think about why your authors have chosen a particular kind of narrator and what effects this enables him/her to achieve. Select different important moments in the text and see how they are affected and enhanced by the choice of narrator.

(iv) Ways of representing thought and speech

This overlaps with the presentation of character and is an area that was developed greatly in 20th century novels. It also overlaps with narrators because there can be a subtle slipping between the narrator's point of view and that of a character as demonstrated under *'free indirect discourse'* below. The main kinds are:

- *Direct speech*, as in the passage from *Pride and Prejudice* above, where the exact words of speech are presented, and the effect can be close to drama.

- *Indirect speech*, where the narrator reports what a character has said without using the exact words, as in 'Mr Bennet replied that he had not'. The effect is a subtle contrast here between Mrs Bennet's active role and Mr. Bennet's passive, distanced one.

- *Free indirect discourse*. This is halfway between the two previous modes, and is the one that makes narrative flexible and rich. It is one of the most important developments in the technique of the novel. Though presented in the third person or omniscient viewpoint, it represents the language and point of view of a character. Jane Austen uses it frequently. Consider:

"Mrs Bennet was quite disconcerted. She could not imagine what business (Mr. Bingley) could have in town so soon after his arrival; and she began to fear that he might always be flying about from one place to another, and never settled at Netherfield as he ought to be."

Halfway through this passage we become conscious that the diction, sentence constructions and point of view has become that of Mrs Bennet. This method is sometimes called the dual voice, as it mixes omniscient narrator and character.

- **Stream of consciousness**.This is the representation of a free, apparently random succession of thoughts and sensations in a character's mind, especially when alone. The first person, 'I' is not used here. The term is often used synonymously with, but is a little different from, interior monologue.

- **Interior monologue**. Here the character is thinking to him/herself *in language*, in words, conscious of what he/she is thinking. Thoughts are formulated in words, whereas in the stream of consciousness they are represented through the narrator.

An awareness of the above techniques should be helpful in the prose commentary and the formal oral, as well as your exam essay. How many of these techniques can you identify in the novels you have read, and what do they contribute?

(v) Character

Character is the jewel in the novel's crown, the thing it does most memorably, its most important element. Though drama consists of characters, the novel can show attitudes towards characters in greater depth and variety, the development of characters through time, and both psychological depth and external interest. Plays can be dramatic without a focus on the individuality of characters, but it is the uniqueness of individual character that makes the novel. Techniques have evolved in the novel writing to express that uniqueness.

Methods of presenting character

Before reading further, think carefully about some of the characters In your novels, listing three or four. Write down some of the moments that reveal them most memorably. Try to account for this. What methods of presentation make those moments stand out?

- Does the narrator describe them? What is the narrator's attitude to them (sympathetic, sympathetic though critical, critical, etc?)

- Is the focus of the description on appearance, moral or social qualities, behaviour, or something else? Are there links between those aspects? If the focus is on appearance, what kinds of elements are described and what clues do these give us about the character?

- Are we given a true and complete impression early on (such as of Mrs Bennet in the first chapter of *Pride and Prejudice*)? Is important information about the character withheld until later (Wickham)? Or is the presentation progressive, revealing more aspects as the novel goes along (Darcy)?

- Are the characters presented mainly through what they do, the decisions they make, or through how and what they think?

- Are the characters revealed through their own, or others' dialogue?

- Do the characters have a particular style of speech? What characterizes this? Is it what they talk about, or how they express themselves, or both, that is striking?

- Are characters presented and illuminated through contrast with another character or characters? What kinds of contrast? Generational, sexual, class, other?

Role or purpose of character

- What does the author seem to want to convey through different characters? (An important moral standpoint, a criticism of unacceptable values or behaviour, a focus on the evolution of the characters' understanding, a representation of an aspect of society, or something else?

43

- What part do minor characters play? Choose several in your texts and find the differences in their function. Do they affect the plot, reveal important information, contrast or pair with one of the main characters, illuminating differences in character or attitude or values? (For example, Charlotte's views on marriage in *Pride and Prejudice* contrast with Elizabeth's.)

(vi) Landscape, setting or place

The 'setting' or context in which a novel takes place, where the geography, or the history, or the social and cultural element may predominate, has always been selected for a reason, and may be used selectively, even distortingly. Certain features will predominate, producing particular effects that have a close relationship with the action and meaning of the novel in question.

Readers are often understandably confused about the concept of setting: it can mean and certainly achieve different things. Kafka's *Metamorphosis* is set in a middle-class apartment described in some detail, in an unidentified bleak city, only vaguely suggested. Both the realistic detail of the apartment and the vagueness of the city create the particular effects Kafka needs. The apartment grounds us in an everyday reality, but the city is disturbingly universal, timeless. Dickens' London settings, by contrast are meticulously described, and can mirror the lives and values of the inhabitants and more broadly the quality of the society. Conrad's Congo is both 'real' and symbolic, suggesting both a real and an inner journey.

Landscape and place may overlap (as in *Wuthering Heights*). On the other hand Jane Austen does not often describe landscape (fields, hills, woods, etc.) in detail. But the sense of place, usually a small community, even specific households, is strongly suggested, and central to Austin's work. Setting may refer to the whole background of a work, or to multiple, different local scenes (the forge, the marshes, Miss Havisham's house in *Great Expectations*). Settings revisited may have a powerful effect, as a measure of the way a character has changed, or of change in the setting itself.

Think of the landscapes or settings (urban, rural, regional) in works you have read. List a few. What features are particularly emphasized? How do they play a part in the work? Remember that landscape and setting may play a variety of roles within the same work.

The variety of roles landscape and setting may play

- Does landscape play a symbolic part in the novel, reflecting character, for example, as in *Wuthering Heights,* or drawing attention to an implicit criticism of the society (the Valley of Ashes in *The Great Gatsby)*?

- Does setting provide a context for social criticism and for encounters with many different kinds of characters, like Huck Finn's river journey and land excursions?

- Does it create tension or dramatic interest, as in the precision of the setting in which the first murder is created in *Crime and Punishment,* or the similar precision of the townscape in *Chronicle of a Death Foretold*?

- Does setting embrace and represent the main character(s), or are they alienated from it, needing to escape and perhaps succeeding, like Huck Finn?

- Is there a shift of seasons in the landscape, reflecting or affecting the action, as in *Tess of the d'Urbervilles*?

- Does landscape or setting permeate the novel, as in *Wide Sargasso Sea*, or is it only important in places?

- Is setting strategic, challenging the characters, causing action or playing a part in the plot (*Lord of the Flies, Chronicle of a Death Foretold*)?

What other roles or effects do landscapes and settings have in your texts?

(vii) Weather

Weather effects can be used in a variety of ways in novels, for example:

- **Strategically** in Jane Austen, as when rain in *Pride and Prejudice* leads to the development of romance between Jane and Bingley, or when Emma finds herself trapped in a coach in a snowstorm with Mr Elton, or when Jane Fairfax excites suspicion for going to collect letters in the rain.

- **Atmospherically**, building suspense as when the great storm in London at Magwich's return in *Great Expectations* signifies the immense upheaval in Pip's life, or the storm builds fear leading to Simon's death in *Lord of the Flies.*

- **Symbolically** as well as atmospherically, as with the constant rain in *A Farewell to Arms*, presaging tragedy, or when lightning strikes the great tree in *Jane Eyre.*

- **Revealing of character,** as in the contributions made by different characters about Jane visiting Netherfield in the rain in *Pride and Prejudice,* or Jane Fairfax risking her health to collect mail in the rain in *Emma.*

Do weather effects occur in your works? What kind of contribution do they make?

(viii) Time

The human obsession with time
Many works of literature, of all genres, are concerned with time, because it is a human obsession and we live in constant awareness of it. Poems may explore a moment in the past, or feelings about time; plays may derive interest from a revelation about the past in connection with one or more character; and autobiography looks at patterns in a life and the significance of past in relation to present. But novels particularly play with the notion of time, moving backwards and forwards in time, distorting chronology in the telling of a story with fascinating effects. Why is this so?

Story, plot and time
When discussing plays we looked at the difference between the chronological story and the way plot highlights connections, cause and effect. This happens even more strikingly in novels. The frequent presence of a narrator means that he or she can move around in mind and memory and connect things as s/he sees fit or appears to 'remember'.

Nick Carraway's story of Gatsby begins after it is all over, and the earliest point in the story – Gatsby's promising boyhood – does not appear until almost the end, where it has an ironic and poignant effect, coming after the tragic events. Juxtaposing such widely separated events (Gatsby's romance with Daisy years ago and their adultery now is another) heightens ironic and tragic perspective. In other cases, where the outcome of the story is told more explicitly early on, we focus more carefully on the 'how' and 'why' of a story, such as *Chronicle of a Death Foretold.* Although we know what will happen, the horror and tragedy of the 'how' is not remotely diminished. As suggested in the Plays section, distinguish plot and chronological 'story' in your texts, and consider the reasons for and effect of some of the order of events or the order of telling of these.

Letters and time
These can be an interesting way of connecting past and present, opening up a new perspective on the past –or revealing a truth about it- as in Darcy's letter to Elizabeth in *Pride and Prejudice.* Much narrative information can be compressed through a letter, facts become dramatic, and it generates an emotional response.

What do I do about new critical thinking about the novel?
It is true that new critical thinking has changed the face of novel criticism in the past thirty years, as indicated in Chapter Three: the Examination Essay. There is, for example, a strong and fascinating interest in the complex relationship between the text and the historic period it was produced in – its values, anxieties, concerns (New Historicism).

Your teachers' discussion, and the critical essays that you and they may read, may well reflect these new approaches, but they do not invalidate traditional approaches. With any text, you need to grasp the basic structure and pattern, the significant themes and issues, the features that bring it to life, and bring your own responses to it. This has not changed.

Bibliography

Your time is limited, the texts come first, and unless you are very selective, critical reading can be confusing. The market is deluged with choice. The following are chosen for their reliability, accessibility and usefulness to you at this stage should you need some background reading or help with texts. But texts first!

Background Reading: The Novel and Short Story, Drama, Poetry

C.W.E.Bigsby. (1984) A Critical Introduction to Twentieth Century American Drama (Three Vols) Cambridge University Press.
Volume Two excellent on Williams, Miller, Albee.

Bradbury, Malcolm (ed.)(1990) *The Novel Today: Contemporary Writers on Modern Fiction.*
Practising novelists write about their own and others' art. Very helpful for those wanting to know about modernism and postmodernism (eg: Kundera and Calvino)

Gilmour, Robin(1986) The Novel in the Victorian Age. Edward Arnold
Said to be one of the best introductions to the Victorian novel.

Innes, Christopher.(1992) Modern British Drama 1890-1990. Cambridge University Press
Detailed discussions of all modern dramatists and movements against their background.

Lodge, David. (1966) The Language of Fiction. Penguin

Lodge, David. (1992) The Art of Fiction, Penguin
Also highly recommended for commentary. Illustrates with extracts and discusses clearly 50 different terms and concepts in fiction. Fascinating and informative.

O'Connor, Frank (1963) The Lonely Voice: A Study of the Short Story
Insights into the genre from a famous practicioner

Perrine, Laurence. (1977) Sound and Sense: An introduction to Poetry.
Excellent, thorough, clear introduction to all major aspects of poetry. Good for commentary

Shaw, Valerie.(1983) The Short Story: A Critical Introduction. Longman
Many detailed references to key writers and texts

Texts about texts: secondary sources (Recommended Series)

Analysing Texts (General Editor Nicolas Marsh) Macmillan: volumes on Bronte, Shakespeare tragedies, Austen, Blake, Forster, Hardy, etc.
Sound and helpful.

Cambridge Companions to Literature. CUP (Volumes on Twain, Beckett, Faulkner, Conrad, Miller, Williams, Chekhov, Dostoievsky etc).
Well worth consulting

Casebooks and New Casebooks. Macmillan.
On a large number of individual authors, provide useful variety of critical approaches to main authors, both classic and contemporary, such as Toni Morrison and Angela Carter

How to Study (ed. John Peck and Martin Doyle) Macmillan Study Guides.
Texts on how to study individual classic authors like Joyce, Conrad, Austen.
Very clear and sound

Longman Critical Essays (Ed. Cookson and Loughrey)
On individual works. Reliable

Penguin Critical Studies (Advisory Editor: Bryan Loughrey) Penguin.
Sound and reliable essays on major individual works of literature

Routledge English Texts (Ed. J. Drakakis)
Good introduction, texts and critical commentary

Routledge Literary Sourcebooks, (Series Editor Duncan Wu) Routledge (Volumes on Frankenstein, Yeats. Keats, Shakespeare, etc.)

Good new series. Introduction to text, context, crucial critical trends, discussion of stage and film adaptations, good analyses of key passages

Writers and their Work, Northcote House in association with The British Council.
This series has a high reputation and includes many contemporary authors as well as classics. Good introduction to context of authors.

Shakespeare

Cambridge Student Guides to Shakespeare Plays, CUP. www.Cambridge.org
There is a great range of 'student guides' to Shakespeare plays, but this really is one of the best. Intelligent and essential commentaries on Acts, different critical approaches, context, guidance on preparing passages, good bibliography

Chapter Three: The Examination Essay

1. Introduction

What should I know about the examination essay?

- It is based on the texts in Part Three of your four-part programme
- It is based on four texts (Higher) three texts (Standard); one of these is World Literature
- It is genre-based: the texts are linked by one genre chosen by your teacher (drama, poetry, novel and short story, or prose non-fiction)
- It is assessed by two-hour examination (H) one-and-a-half hour (S)
- It is worth 25% of your final grade

When is it studied?

Teachers may begin these texts in the first year, but often teach them in the second year, nearer to the examination. In this case it may be helpful to read at least some of them ahead of time. In the pressured months before the exam, it is easy to run out of time to study carefully. Some personal strategies for both studying and revising appropriately are given in Chapter Two: How to Study Texts. You need time to revise, and time to *compare* texts once you have read them all.

What does the exam paper look like?

It is very important to familiarise yourself with the layout of the exam paper and the kinds of questions asked. Your teacher should provide you with copies of past questions and papers. Higher and Standard level papers have a similar format and very similar questions.

There is a section for each genre, with two questions in it. You choose *one* of these questions only, from the genre you have studied. There is also a 'General Section' with a choice of further questions. You may choose a question from this section *instead* of your genre section but you must use your Part Three texts and choose a question that suits your genre. You are expected to write on two of your texts, or at most three.

As each school chooses its texts (from a list of prescribed authors) the questions are designed to be answered in relation to a great variety of works, not specific texts.

What are the particular skills I should have for the exam essay?

To a large extent, you need the same skills and qualities for the exam essay that you need for the other assessed components, such as:

- A good understanding of the works
- Detailed and appropriate references to the works
- A recognition and appreciation of literary features
- A clear, focused, logical, and well-supported argument
- Precise, grammatical and effective use of language

In addition, there is a criterion unique to this paper: Response to the Question. This requires you to understand the specific demands of the question, and to show relevance, critical thinking and detailed illustration in your address of the question. This is the weakest aspect of performance in the exam essay, closely followed by discussion of literary features.

How can I develop these skills?

- A *good understanding* may be developed, apart from class teaching, by studying the strategies outlined in this and the previous chapter (How to Study Texts).
- Ways to make *detailed references* and provide *a clear argument* are illustrated in this chapter and the chapter on World Literature.

- The two problem areas, the *appreciation of literary features* and the *addressing of the question*, are dealt with in some detail below.
- *Good writing* is the result of much reading and frequent practice in writing. Some teachers require, for example, a piece of written work at least every two weeks. Putting thought and care into these essays and attending to teacher comments will certainly stand you in good stead. There tends to be a strong correlation between typical achievement in these essays, and performance in the exam.

  Making the effort to write good notes that express your responses and ideas concisely is an excellent way to develop your written expression. Listening thoughtfully to class discussion and making the effort to participate, to express your thoughts, will also help your writing, as will discussing the works with friends. However, you may not be given a lot of practice in exam essays, so pay attention to what is required, as illustrated below

2. Problem areas in the exam essay: literary features

What are they?

This is an important question. Students and even teachers can be confused about what literary features are. Knowing what they are is the first step to writing about them appropriately.

Basically the phrase is very inclusive, embracing all the means by which authors give shape and significance and meaning and individuality to their works (for example: structure, setting, narrative perspective, methods of characterisation, dialogue, images and symbols, language and style). Although there is some overlap between the genres, such as characterization, structure, language, and so on, there are also features specific to, or particularly important in individual genres.

For example there are specifically *dramatic* or theatrical features in plays (such as lighting and sound effects, entrances and exits, amongst others) that create meaning and impact in real or imagined performance, and would come under the heading of 'literary features'. In novels the choice of narrator, the perspective and voice are very important, but are rarely relevant to drama. Literary features of poetry and prose are also listed and described in Chapter One: The Exam Commentary, Chapter Two: How to Study Texts, and the Glossary.

How do I incorporate discussion of these features into my essay, showing 'response to effects'?

It is a first and essential step to know what the concept 'literary features' means, and to be able to identify individual features in works. The response to the *effects* of these, and the ability to discuss them, must come from a close and careful reading of texts such as is shown further on in this chapter and the previous chapter. You need to reach the point where you know the text so well, and have entered into the life of it, that these features are an integral part of your reading and your awareness. An example of what this means should help.

Read the following carefully. It is part of the body of an essay on the question provided, giving an example of the discussion of one text. It is recommended that you read it once through for general understanding, perhaps jotting some responses in the margin, then more closely. On the second reading, *decide where literary features are being discussed, and what these are*, by pencilling numbers in the text as you read and identifying the features in the margin.

A sample showing discussion of literary features in a drama essay (from the middle of the essay)

> *"Openings and endings of plays, though separated by upheavals and changes in the lives of the characters, are often closely connected in effect. Discuss and compare how far you have found this true of two or three plays you have studied."*

The opening of A Streetcar Named Desire shows Blanche's arrival at her sister's apartment in New Orleans. The ending shows her forced departure from this apartment, with her sister and brother-in-law and their new baby in sole possession of their home once more. Between these two points Blanche's gradual loss of grip on her sanity, exacerbated by Stan's opposition to her, has been enacted. The connection, the similarity between beginning and end, is Blanche, and the apartment. This pattern reflects a classic structure effectively used by many dramatists: the entry of a character into a stable situation (here, a husband and pregnant wife in their home), which challenges that situation and must lead to the change or departure of one or more of the characters. In this case, the stable situation is regained after the disruption of the outsider. Blanche has to go, if the unity of the family is to be kept.

This structure, however, gives us a clue to the differences between opening and ending. The first image in the opening is Blanche, incongruous in white, and moth-like, against the noisy modern urban background of New Orleans; the last image (after Blanche's exit) is two-fold – the men playing poker, and Stan soothing Stella, who is cradling her new baby but also sobbing. Stan is unbuttoning her blouse in a characteristically sexual gesture. The sexual relationship is the strong heart of their marriage, but will it be enough to keep them together after what has happened? The ending brings unease rather than a sense of settling back into stability. Blanche was not just an 'outsider', she is also a sister, and the bond between the sisters was strong.

In the case of both opening and ending, the power of the image or tableau is strong and conveys much of the meaning. However, our reaction to these is quite different and is much stronger at the end than at the beginning. At the beginning, the first image or impression is of the Elysian Fields quarter of New Orleans. This setting is important because it is into this environment that Blanche will come in a few moments, an environment where she will never feel at home and will feel snobbishly alienated from because the Old, 'aristocratic' South of her background, is her identity, even if it is degenerate and in decline. This alienation will fuel the hostility between her and her brother-in-law Stanley, the new, urban second-generation 'Polack' American. Yet the setting is also attractive, if poor, with its lively piano music and the 'easy intermingling of races'. We can understand why Stella and Stan are happy here, and cannot entirely sympathise with Blanche's rejection of it. It is part of an opposition of two worlds, the old and the new, at the heart of the play, each with some appealing qualities.

The atmosphere of the evening is 'lyrical', the sky a 'tender blue', so that when Blanche appears on the scene, dramatically contrasting with it in her white suit and jewellery, hat and gloves, there is something almost romantic which arouses our interest and expectations. Because she is out of place and uncertain, she appears vulnerable. Only later do we understand that she is both like and unlike a moth, tough in some of the things she has done, fragile because of things that have happened to her. Her final exit connects with this because, though mentally shaken, she displays a last show of dignity in her clothes and manner and speech, our final image of her, and so a sympathetic one. But the last image of all is the disconcerting one. Although the play has led us to see that this household, this marriage, cannot be shared, and that Blanche's past cannot simply be wiped out, Stan's 'victory' is an unpleasant one, and Stella's apparent complicity equally unsettling. We feel alienated from them. Blanche has come between us and them. We know too much about her now to accept this solution without feelings.

Before proceeding at this point, check that you have carried out the instructions above the extract.

Some of the features you should have found are:

- **Openings and endings**: Exam questions quite often involve the discussion of a specific literary feature
- A sense of the **structure** of the whole play, the pattern the action forms (paragraph 1)
- Visual **images** (figure in a setting; tableau at the end)
- The **presentation of character through clothes, colour, speech and appearance** (paragraph 2 and 4)
- The presentation of character through 'characteristic **gesture**' (paragraph 2)
- **Setting** describing the role both of New Orleans and the 'quarter' (paragraph 2 and 3)
- **Contrast**: New America and Old South, as in Stan and Blanche (paragraph 3)
- **Sound**: the 'blue piano' lively and atmospheric music; the street cries and voices (paragraph 3).
- **Lighting and atmosphere**: the tender blue of the sky (paragraph 4)
- **Language, metaphor and symbol** – the 'moth' (paragraph 2)

It will probably surprise you that ten features have quite effortlessly been incorporated into a four-paragraph discussion focusing on the comparison and contrast of openings and endings. The candidate is probably not even conscious of trying to include them, but his response to and engagement with the play, his need to bring it alive to the reader in order to illustrate his point, naturally draws upon the features of the play that are memorable and bear meaning.

And that's how it should be. When you have engaged with your texts in a similar manner, by reading the texts well and using the strategies proposed throughout this Guide, and if you do not take short cuts by using 'cribs' or study notes that seem to do the work for you, you will find yourself referring to and analysing features without worrying about it too much. What you want to avoid is answering the question briefly, and then, using a 'shopping list' of various features you have memorised, trying to apply these to the text.

Some ways to revise for 'features' in the exam

Take each of the ten aspects listed in the analysis above and consider if and how they function in relation to your own texts. Look carefully for contrasting or different ways in which they function within the same text, and in different texts compared.

Then consider further aspects of plays, such as these:

Portable objects or 'props': (For example, the tape-recorder, the pen Biff steals in *Salesman*; the clock broken in *Three Sisters*; do they have any symbolic or wider meaning?

Violence: How is it used and what effect does it have? Is it on or offstage?

Time: What kind of time are we made aware of and how? Is the action working against the clock, creating suspense, threatening change?

Space: Do spatial relations between characters or parts of the set have importance?

Entrances and exits: How has the writer used these for particular effects?

Secondary or minor characters: What role do they play? What effects are achieved by introducing them?

How to analyse effects in detail

When you know the text well, it is easier to discuss it in detail, so knowing the text is a first stage. Second, in answering a question such as the one above, you need to select clear details to illustrate your point. Proving the point persuasively will involve 'analysis' or further discussion of these details.

For example, a point made in the above extract is that the New Orleans setting (a literary feature) is an important aspect of the opening of the play, and has an impact on the outcome of the play. If you simply make that statement it's a start, but no more. Even just remembering some of the details of the setting is not enough. You need to see them in relation to the whole play and its evolution.

To develop your point, ask yourself these kinds of questions:
Why is the setting important? How does it have that 'impact on the ending'?
Ideas might be as follows:

* Because of the way it looks (charming and sympathetic- it affects us positively and sensuously through its appeal to senses of sight and sound)

* Because of what it stands for (the New America versus the Old South- an idea we only understand as we absorb the whole play)

* Because it is the new and alien environment that will test Blanche (which we see immediately she appears, and through the play)

    Perhaps you can think of other reasons too

Each of these answers now needs to be expanded and supported by close references to the text (in both its details and as a whole). In doing that, you have analysed a 'feature' and reached perhaps the highest mark for that assessment criterion. How hard was that?

A sample illustrating discussion of features in a novel essay (from the beginning of the essay)

51

As with the drama essay above, read this through carefully identifying where literary features are referred to and discussed.

The novel has always been associated with travel and mobility. For what purposes and to what effects do novelists you have studied use journeys? Compare two or three works.

In life we often make journeys because of the pleasure of going somewhere new, and the stimulation of sights and experiences along the way. In novels the reasons for journeys and the ways in which they function are far more strategic, complex and revealing. They may for example facilitate the change, development or social mobility of a character; they may enable the author to pass social comment on the various people or events experienced on route; or they may create suspense and concern for characters through the adventures or difficulties encountered. Indeed, a single novel may encompass all of these elements.

It is the treatment of these elements, however, that provides the interest and makes one text about a journey so different from another. Conrad's Heart of Darkness and Steinbeck's The Grapes of Wrath both describe long and difficult journeys that test the characters and comment critically on aspects of their societies. Both do this in such a way that we feel closely involved with the characters in their progress, notably through the choice of narrative viewpoint and the use of images and concrete details, but these work differently in each case.

At the beginning of The Grapes of Wrath we are presented with a strong sense of the Oklahoma farmlands where the three generations of the Joad family and others have lived their lives, and from which they are forced to move. Their journey means uprooting and displacement and initially takes its poignance from the sense of what they have to leave behind, creating anger in readers against the capitalists who have helped bring about the situation, and engaging our emotions, so that we feel concern for them as they prepare for their long journey. An omniscient viewpoint allows us to feel this loss through a variety of perspectives. There are Tom's memories as he comes 'home' to a ruin, and his eyes (which are our eyes too) move over the features of the homestead, remembering family life there. There are Muley's memories of his life, described round the campfire, which are so strong that he would rather live as an outcast than move. And there is the generalised point of view of men and women in that community selecting the few items they can take, in the stream of consciousness intercalary chapters. The men linger over farm implements that were like old friends, and the harnesses of beloved horses, before bitterly selling them for a pittance; the women ponder family momentos – a book, an ornament, a letter, before abandoning them. "How can we live without our lives? How will we know it's us without our past?" Such personal details and sense of place connect us with the characters and make their difficult journey into the unknown real to us.

Conrad's Marlow begins his more exotic and remote journey from a very different standpoint, as going to Africa is for him the accomplishment of a dream he has had since boyhood. However, the details surrounding his going, with their symbolic overtones and surreal, almost nightmarish descriptions provide an ominous foreshadowing of danger, and even more of death. Brussels is a 'whited sepulchre' to him, a powerful allusion simultaneously to Christ's condemnation of the hypocritical ('whited') Pharisees and ironically to the Belgian Empire sending its 'emissaries of light' into the savage darkness. The grass growing up through the cobblestone streets of this apparently thriving capital seems contradictory but is also an eerie reminder of the description of Marlow's predecessor in the Congo, Fresleven, killed by natives in revenge and later found by Marlow with the grass growing up through his (presumably whitened) bones. Grass, the sinister symbol of time and mortality already begins to suggest the futility of man's accomplishments in such enterprises. The indifference of the fateful knitting women in the company's offices, and the cynicism of the doctor suggest the cheapness of life, the lack of value attached to it as it streams out to Africa. The retrospective tale, sharpening these images, emphasizes the vulnerability and ignorance of the young 'hero' as he sets off on the journey that will change him forever.

Before proceeding at this point, check that you have carried out the exercise suggested at the start of the essay.

Some of the features you should have found are:

- *Journeys:* As with the drama essay, questions themselves often involve the discussion of a literary feature

- *Suspense:* The characters set out on their journeys with misgivings (introduction, paragraphs 3 and 4)

- **Narrative viewpoint:** The advantages of the omniscient narrator and the first person narrator are discussed in paragraphs 3 and 4 respectively

- **A sense of place:** This is suggested in some detail in paragraph 3 describing the homestead, and more briefly in paragraph 4 describing Brussels

- **Stream of consciousness:** The reason for using this and the effects created by it are discussed at the end of paragraph 3 together with details from an early example in the novel

- **'Intercalary' chapters:** A famous device in this novel, but used in other works too, the chapters are a counterpoint to the main narrative, providing a broader national and historical perspective showing the plight of other similar generalized characters (paragraph 3)

- **Details:** Concrete details and images, their meaning and effects, are discussed in paragraphs 3 and 4. Both novels are full of images but they function differently in each case

- **Metaphors and symbols:** These may be fused (the "whited sepulchre" is both metaphor and symbol) or separate –grass is both concrete and symbolic

- **Allusion:** The "whited sepulchre" (paragraph 4)

- **Flash forward / chronology / foreshadowing:** The mention of Marlow's predecessor Fresleven in paragraph 4 both looks back, to an earlier point in the story before Marlow's journey, and forward to the moment he will find his bones during his journey. The positioning of this incident before the journey begins foreshadows the effect that Africa will have

- **Contrast:** Light and dark imagery and symbolism (paragraph 4)

- **Dual perspective:** We are both aware of the young Marlow / hero setting off on his journey, and the older Marlow telling the tale retrospectively. This creates a complexity and Irony of effect

At least twelve features have been effortlessly referred to within these paragraphs. The candidate has identified *two main features* through which he will explore the meaning of journeys (*Images* and *narrative viewpoint*) and this section of the essay deals in some detail with both of these features. In the course of discussing these two elements, other features, such as the stream of consciousness and symbols, are inevitably referred to.

Appreciation and detailed analysis of effects in the above sample

The candidate clearly feels moved by the loss of the Joads' home and way of life. 'Strong sense' and 'poignance' (paragraph 3) indicate a response, which is then supported by details about the objects the farmers had to leave behind. Similes 'like old friends' and adjectives like 'beloved' horses, show that the reader has entered sympathetically into the life of the novel and its characters. Emotions are not involved in the same way in *Heart of Darkness,* but there is an appreciation for the way in which images work symbolically creating atmosphere and meaning, rather as in poetry. These images and details are identified and explained, while the adjectives the candidate uses, like 'surreal', 'nightmarish' and 'sinister', show that he has understood and responded to the connotations of the imagery.

Some ways to revise for novel, short story, and non-fiction features in the exam

In addition to what has been illustrated here, you should look carefully at Chapter Two: How to Study Texts, for a description of some of the most important features and techniques found in novels and short stories, which overlap to some extent with non-fiction. Further ways of approaching non-fiction are listed in Chapter Four: Internal (Oral) Assessment.

3. Revising for the poetry question in the exam

There will normally be at least three stages in your study of poetry in the course of your programme for the exam:

- A study of the individual poems of each author, their meaning and characteristics
- A consideration of how the individual poems fit into the 'oeuvre' or body of the poet's work, including something of the life of the poet and how far this affected the direction of the poems
- Some comparative work, based on exam questions, comparing for example the use of images in different poems and poets, or the effects of structure or tone

For the purposes of the exam, the first and third are particularly important. There are four ways you can ensure these stages are covered well:

(i)   Go carefully through the poetry section of Chapter One on Commentary to ensure you can identify significant features of poetry and can discuss their effects. Go through the glossary too, and other resources like the ones listed in the bibliography.

(ii) Be very familiar with a number of your individual poems so that you can discuss them from any angle and quote from them to illustrate a variety of topics. Your essay will be entirely based on a discussion of a selection of your poems, so this is the most fundamental way you can prepare yourself for the exam. Read your poems aloud, as if communicating them to others, thinking about tone, the effects of sound, pauses and pacing, and what these contribute.

(iii) Take a selection of poems (let us say, seven or eight) including several different authors and find ways of linking them. You may find surprising connections and this will help you explore them in new and flexible ways. It will also get you into the habit of working comparatively.

For example, you might find that several use rhyme in interesting and different ways, or that they use water imagery for different purposes, or that they conclude in unexpected ways, or that they have a strong speaking voice. Some will connect perhaps in several ways, others in only one or apparently not at all. It is more interesting and dynamic if you can work with a partner or in a group doing this, as you'll find more links. Don't start with a preconceived idea or list of things to look out for. Approaching the exercise with an open mind will increase your flexibility.

(iv) Finally, consider the following topics, and select three or four poems representing two or three different poets studied, which you might use to develop an answer:

The voice in the poem - What impact can this have? Does it establish a compelling personality as in Donne or Browning? Does it connect with the reader, drawing us in to share the experience? How far do male and female voices differ? Compare different effects of voice.

A regional context - Some poets are identified with a particular area. What relationship do they have with it? What features do they emphasise? How do they make the physical aspects of the region come alive for us?

Dominant emotions - What are some of the dominant emotions you have found in a number of your poems (pity, anger, tenderness, regret, delight, etc.)? Compare some of the ways these emotions function. What means are used to express and emphasize them?

Narrative - Some poems narrate an incident – a moment in war, perhaps, or an illuminating domestic or personal moment. For what purposes are such incidents used in some of your poems? What means are employed to bring the incident alive? What kinds of response do they evoke in us?

Imagery - Look at some of the different ways in which imagery is used. Select a range of images from different poems and compare their function and impact.

Contrast / tension - Look back at Chapter One on commentary for a discussion of the ways contrast or tension can be used in poems. Find some striking contrasts in a selection of your poems and compare the ways these are established and the part they play in the meaning of the poem.

Structure - How are some of your poems structured and what effects come from that structure?

Sound - Sound effects can be very powerful in poetry, especially as it is generally meant to be heard. How do some of your poets create sound effects and for what purposes? Through diction, alliteration, metre and rhyme, or other ways? (Consult the Glossary for more.)

Again, working with a friend or in a small group can be very helpful in working through these topics.

4. Problem areas in the exam essay: answering the question

There are several possible reasons why candidates often don't focus on the question, and so lose marks. Which of these might be yours?

- They don't know the texts well enough, or haven't studied them in the ways suggested in this guide, which help you focus on the most significant aspects

- They haven't developed sufficient flexibility of mind to turn their knowledge to any question asked (Chapter Two: Studying Texts shows you how to do this). This comes with practice and is closely related to the next reason

- They haven't practised reading exam questions carefully and analysing them. This involves (a) breaking the question down into parts, identifying the tasks you are being asked to do; (b) identifying key words or phrases that are the clues to the focus needed; (c) seeing how to relate the question to the text (asking the right questions about the texts)

- They are determined to offload what they have memorized or what they know, regardless of the precise terms of the question. They feel that the question doesn't allow them to show enough of what they know

- They may have read the texts, but haven't revised them, so they don't have a clear overall view of them from which to select relevant aspects

(i) Looking at the paper: panic and the frightening question

Candidates often panic when they see the questions, because they may not have seen questions worded exactly like that, and may feel they haven't 'studied' that aspect of their works or been specifically prepared for that. In addition, questions may contain challenging quotations or statements that require you to think in new ways, 'on your feet'. It is quite normal to react in this way, although if you have experienced a number of 'mock' exams, and worked through questions papers, this is not so frightening. If you have studied your texts in the ways suggested, and know your texts well, you should be able to turn your mind to any aspect of them, to any question you are asked, regardless of whether you have discussed, written about or revised this precise aspect.

The examiner wants to see how you can *think*, not how much knowledge you can show on a prepared topic. You may feel that you are not getting the opportunity to show what you really know about a text, by narrowing your answer to what is asked, but the relevance of the way you answer the question is all-important. Nothing irritates an examiner as much as irrelevance, and you get no credit for it.

(ii) Identifying the parts and focus of the question

To understand clearly how to do this, look at the following example and carry out the instructions:

> *Compare and contrast the presentation of any three or four characters in plays you have studied. Say how, and how effectively, each character seems to you to further the dramatic force of the play in which he or she appears (May 2001, H)*

What are the key words or phrases here, which indicate what you need to focus on?
What words or concepts might you need to define before planning an answer?
Turn the whole question into a series of questions that make your task clear.

```
1.
2
3
4
```

Key phrases or words might be identified as 'compare and contrast', 'presentation', 'dramatic force' 'how', 'how effectively'. You might need to define 'presentation' and 'dramatic force' for yourself before you move on. Your questions might look like this:

- How are A, B and C (your choice of characters) 'presented'? In other words, what methods are used to make them vivid and particular to us? How far are these methods similar or dissimilar in different texts?
- How do these characters contribute to the dramatic action of the play they appear in?
- How effective is this contribution? (ie: how do I respond to this action? How does it engage my interest?)

(iii) Planning an answer

Answering these questions as part of your plan might involve something like this:
- First, jot down your plays and think about each for a moment (candidates sometimes forget what is on their Part Three list).
- Decide which characters might make the best examples and sketch out some ideas. You would want to have some contrasts.

Supposing I don't understand exactly what is meant by a word or phrase like 'presentation'?

You need to decide what you think it means, and stick to your definition. It is true that the idea of "presentation" here isn't entirely clear. Does it just mean 'introduced' to us at the outset, when the characters first appear, or more generally as shown through the play? Decide which probably works best. For example, if you only looked at Nora as she is first presented to us in the first pages of *A Doll's House*, you would have a distorted impression of her, as Torvald does. Surely the fact that we see at least two sides of her is part of the way she is 'presented'. So the more general approach would work best here.

(iv) The need to address all parts of the question; the importance of 'how?'

Questions always test your knowledge of 'how' as well as 'what', expecting you to address not only '*what* is this character like?' but '*how* does he or she contribute to the impact of the play?'

A common weakness of candidates in answering this kind of question is to focus on a word or idea or section of the question they feel comfortable with (in this case, probably 'character') and rush blindly into giving three or four little character studies, without any 'argument' or discussion.

5. Ten frequently asked questions about the exam

Is there any danger in taking a question from the General Section?

The answer is both yes and no. The general questions are designed to meet the needs of any genre studied, but some may be more applicable to your genre and course of study than others. You need to be very careful, in choosing a question from this section, that it really is suited to your genre and does allow you to use the texts you have read to best advantage. Some questions may be directed to those who have some special knowledge of an area –for example, literary theory or biography, or offer a particular challenge that might only be appropriate to a minority of candidates. You should not take these if you do not have sufficient background or are not really sure what the question requires.

On the other hand, it may well be the case that a question on the General Section may be more interesting and appropriate to your study than the questions in your particular genre section, and in that case, you should take advantage of it.

How much time should I take to plan? What is the best way to do this?

You have seven questions to look through, two on your genre section and five in the general section. Do not waste time looking through other sections. You need to move on to the planning stage, which might take twenty minutes to half an hour, whether you are Higher or Standard Level. Some candidates start writing almost immediately, which is very dangerous practice.

Once you have selected the question you think you can answer best (and analysed it by breaking it down into parts, as demonstrated above), you need to focus on a clear line of approach that will guide you right through your essay. This will be defined in your opening paragraph. To come up with this line, think first of your texts, and let these be the basis for your approach. Always work from the concrete and particular illustration to the general statement. Don't try to think in generalities first.

For example, if you had selected the question on openings and endings of plays, as provided in the box above, you should think first of the plays in your Part Three programme and ask yourself these kinds of questions:

What are their openings and endings exactly?
What response did I have to these?
What pattern does each of them have?
How alike or different are they?
Which two or three will work best and provide the most interesting comparison?

Once you have worked out some answers to these questions, and structured the ideas clearly, you might come up with something like this candidate.

> *Openings and endings of plays often have interesting patterns. They may show the same group of characters in the same setting, but emphasise some difference or effect that reflects what has happened, as in* Three Sisters *or* Master Harold and the Boys. *Or the setting may have a character missing, as in* A Streetcar Named Desire. *But an essential difference between our response to the beginning and the end is that by the end, we know the characters, and often care about them and their situation, so that our response to the ending is likely to be stronger and more complex than to the opening. That response may be to a wider issue, such as racism in* Master Harold, *or to a family situation as in* Three Sisters, *or to a specific central character, as in* Streetcar.

What makes a good opening paragraph or introduction?

We can see from this example that the candidate has worked out some clear differences, which will form the basis of the comparison he will develop, and from thinking about these, has come up with a clear line of thought about the more complex response to endings. The comparative structure will be his anchor to the question as he moves through his detailed discussion. It will also firmly link the different sections on different plays, so that they don't become unconnected mini-essays on separate texts. Look back at the middle section on *Streetcar* in the box earlier, to see how he connects discussion of the play to the thesis at the beginning.

Opening paragraphs do not have to be clever or profound. Although there is no one formula for them, they should be relevant, clearly related to your texts, and show a distinct line of 'attack'. There are similarities to the introductions to World Literature assignments here. They should quickly lead into a discussion of your texts, without 'padding' or 'waffling'. A good introduction is rarely more than half a page long. The complexity, the real interest of your work, lies in the development of your ideas in your middle section or body of your essay. There are several good examples of opening paragraphs in this chapter that you can use as models – in section 2 above (literary features) and section 8 below (sample essays).

57

Although you need to sketch out some of the important details and ideas you want to use for each text, don't spend *too* much time on this in the planning stage. if you know your works well, much will come to you as you are writing, and you may find your discussion becoming more complex as you go along. The examiner marks your essay, not the plan. Your conclusion will arise out of this discussion and may include ideas that you did not foresee at the beginning.

How much should I write? How many texts should I discuss?

You cannot discuss two or three texts *in detail* in two or three sides. Although it somewhat depends on the conciseness of your style, and the size of your handwriting, five to six sides is more reasonable, as illustrated below. Some candidates write much more.

As to how many texts you should tackle: for Standard Level, with only just over an hour for the actual writing, covering two texts discussed in detail is manageable. If you try to cover three, you may not be able to write about each in sufficient detail, and the detail is important. The same goes for Higher Level. Much depends on the speed with which you think and write. Very good answers have been produced using both two and three texts. It all depends on the quality of your ideas and the depth of your discussion.

Should I prepare quotes?

On the whole, if you know your texts well (in the case of fiction, drama and non-fiction) you will be able to refer closely to relevant parts, perhaps even quoting a remembered phrase or sentence, and this will be sufficient. You cannot guess what will be relevant to the exam questions, and learning quotes in anticipation may make you want to include them at all costs, which can lead you into irrelevance. It is concise and relevant *detail* that is important. Look back at your samples in section 2 of this chapter for examples of such detail.

Poetry is another matter. The quantity of text is much less and the ability to quote lines and phrases in support of ideas is *expected* in this case. Read the poems aloud, preferably with a friend, thinking about them as wholes, so that you can discuss them from any angle, and quote to answer any question. In addition, it is helpful to prepare some quotes, but note the advice above about using prepared quotes at any cost.

How should I structure my essay? Taking each text in turn, or illustrating each main point from each text?

This is a question that is also addressed in the World Literature section and the answer is similar. It can work either way, depending on how you set up the argument in your introduction. It is this argument, which should indicate lines of comparison and contrast, which will hold the essay together. (See the essay samples below on drama and the novel).

How do I avoid telling the story?

Telling the story is a frequent weakness in exam essays. The examiner is expected to know the texts. If you have followed the analytical method of reading and revising texts, as outlined in the previous chapter How To Study Texts, and if you follow the analytical approach to addressing the question, as described in this chapter, you are likely to avoid this approach. Focus on the question and what it is asking, illustrating with the best examples you can think of.

If I have never done a 'mock' or an essay of this kind, can I still do well on the exam?

It is obviously preferable to have had practice and to learn from that. If you have not had that opportunity, however, there is no need for despair. If you are a good reader, have read widely, and follow carefully the suggestions for studying texts and approaching the exam, as provided in this chapter and the previous one, there is no reason why you should not succeed.

Should I read secondary sources to help me understand my texts better?

On the whole, reading your texts carefully, making notes and following the strategies recommended here (in addition to class teaching discussion) should be sufficient to ensure good performance and are essential. 'Study Aids' should never be used as an alternative to the above stages of study.

However, school situations vary and you may feel you need more help. A good introduction to a text (such as to the Penguin editions), providing some biographical information and an indication of an author's tendencies, pre-occupations and intentions (as far as these can be defined), is essential. Take an A4 sheet and jot down the most illuminating comments by the author, a few reputable critics and perhaps the editor of your text in relation to each of your Part Three texts.

Some reliable critical studies are listed at the end of Chapter Two but should be used with caution. They may only confuse you or take too long to read. You should only embark on these if you feel secure enough in your own reading of your texts to be able to view another's ideas alongside your own. Using the internet can be more time-consuming than it is worth and sources need to be checked with care, though it can of course yield helpful material. Remember, the text comes first.

Should I know about literary theory or approaches?

This question applies to the study of novels more than to other genres. The simple answer is that you do not need to know specifically about these in order to do very well on the exam. Your careful and responsive study of texts, as emphasized everywhere in this guide, should prepare you for success, and may not leave you with much time for mastering the various critical "approaches".

As noted in the answer to the question above on choosing from the General Section of the exam paper, a question in that section may well draw upon explicit knowledge of "reading approaches". These involve textual approaches such as "Structuralism"; contextual approaches such as the sociological; "New Historicism", the postcolonial, the biographical and the psychological; and ideological approaches such as Marxist and feminist.

Explicitly or implicitly, your teacher may have drawn on several of these approaches, even when studying a single text, and some of the reputable secondary sources referred to in the bibliography in Chapter Two such as the *New Casebooks* series, will include essays drawing on different approaches. It is both interesting and stimulating, but not essential, to study these approaches specifically at this level. On the other hand, some of these approaches are part of what seems a 'normal' and even essential study of a work (for example the "contextual" - the study of the historical and cultural context in which the work was written) so that you may not even realize you are using an "approach".

However, there is also a danger that without adequate guidance, readings of texts can be distorted, and this could be a disadvantage to you. No text at this stage should be approached through one perspective only. Balance is required, and some approaches are best used only when you have a thorough basic grasp of the text yourself, using the kinds of strategies outlined in the previous chapter. You will have to be the judge of how far you have the time, ability and motivation to pursue this. If you do, there are some excellent books to help you understand this area of study.

6. Some ways to prepare for the exam (in addition to re-reading the texts)

- Going back through earlier notes only has limited value and should never be used as a substitute for revising the texts. However, it's a good idea to go back through them and draw together, preferably on one or two sheets only, the notes and ideas you think might be most helpful so that you have these all in one place. Your most recent revision notes should show a better and more complex understanding than those of a year ago, but many earlier notes may still be valid.

- Go through Chapter Two: How to Study Texts, and think about literary features in relation to your Part Three genre.

- Look back through a number of your past essays, including 'mock' exams if you have done these. What comments has your teacher made? Is there a pattern to these comments? If your teacher has used the criteria for the exam essay in his/her marking, what are the weaker areas? Are there any grammatical, punctuation or spelling errors you have made consistently? Make a list of the areas of difficulty on a single A4 sheet, so as to avoid repeating any of these errors or tendencies.

- Take some past papers or questions that you have not worked through. (Your teacher may do this with you in class, of course). With a friend or by yourself, follow the recommended procedure above for reading questions and planning how best to answer them. Use the texts to re-read relevant sections.

- Read carefully through the assessment criteria for the exam essay. Highlight the parts that could prove a challenge for you and decide on some strategies to help you.

- Read the following sample essays, so that you understand the standards expected.

- Above all, RE-READ THE TEXTS.

7. Some further tips for the exam room

- Be clear which texts are on your Part Three list. Candidates can be hazy about this. The exam paper does say that you can use a Part Two (Detailed Study) text *in addition to* detailed discussion of two of your Part Three texts. Consider the points made in the paragraph above on how many works to discuss, before you do this. It can be a nice way to use a text you have enjoyed in Part Two but not had a chance to use. However, the bulk of your essay should be on Part Three.

- Check that you know and can spell the titles of your texts and the characters in them.

- Clearly indicate which question you are answering. It can be a good idea to write the question out, so that you keep it firmly in your mind throughout (though some teachers may say that writing it out wastes time).

- Keep a balance in your discussion of your texts. Give them more or less equal treatment.

- If your teachers have complained about the difficulty of reading your handwriting, don't suppose that the examiner will find it any easier. Double space your writing, use a pen that writes clearly, and take a little trouble to write more carefully. The examiner only has about fifteen minutes to spend on your paper (yes, even after your years of work). If he or she has to puzzle out what you are saying, this may have a negative effect.

- If you 'white out' words or sections of sentences, do go back and fill in the blanks. You are not penalized for crossing something out neatly and writing a correction over the top.

- Make sure that you can spell words and understand grammatical constructions that your teachers may have been correcting on your essays for years. Although you are not penalized for the odd error, frequent mistakes are going to pull your grade down. Take time at the end to read through your essay carefully and correct mistakes.

- Do break up your argument into clear paragraphs. Unbroken pages of prose are disheartening for the examiner, and can lose you marks on Criteria C (Presentation) and D (Use of Language). Poor paragraphing indicates an inability to think clearly and organize your thoughts. Look at the discussion on how to paragraph in the World Literature chapter.

- Don't rush through the writing to 'get it over with' (candidates *do* do this sometimes). You have taken two years –and more- to get to this point. Do justice to yourself.

8. Samples of exam essays

Sample One: Drama (Higher Level)

You will see from the following Higher Level question that it could equally serve any of the genres: poetry, prose, or drama. Read it with the assessment criteria to hand, but first noting what seems to you effective and strong. Identifying strong qualities will help you move towards these in your own work.

"Contrasts of light and darkness, either literal or metaphorical, have proven a rich source for both visual artists and writers. Compare and contrast how far works you have studied have used this resource to good effect."

The opposing elements of light and darkness are frequently used in literature, both as a stage effect and as a symbolic portrayal of the conflicts and oppositions between characters, or even inside characters as they struggle between two opposing forces. Western culture has inherited the Greek idea of duality, and the balance of light and dark is often a metaphorical illustration of other powerful opposites, good and evil, pleasure and pain, truth and illusion, knowledge and ignorance.

In Euripides' <u>Medea</u>, this metaphorical opposition is used to dramatic effect. The conflict of a symbolic 'light and dark' is clear in the struggle of love versus hate, as well as right versus wrong. The fierce drive for revenge that Medea feels, struggles with her love for her children, and we see the inner pain this causes in her dramatic monologues, where she is torn between love for her children, and the need to hurt Jason. The chorus asks her, 'Can you steel your heart?', and she feels that she can, and that she must, in order to 'deal Jason the deepest wound'. As the dreadful moment 'that will test my nerve' draws near, though, she begins to waver, or 'weaken', as she sees it. As the chorus have said, 'Your heart will melt. You will know you cannot', and she does indeed feel incapable of committing such an 'unholy deed'. Yet, she must master her emotions in order to avenge her pride: it is a kind of heroic duty for her. She reminds herself of the necessity of carrying out the murder, demanding of herself, 'Are my enemies to laugh at me?'

The struggle that she faces, one moment veering towards one decision, the next resolving to do the other, shows the duality of her nature - and human nature in general - between 'light' and 'dark'. In the end, it is the dark anger that wins out: 'I understand the horror of what I am about to do, but anger, the source of all life's horror, masters my resolve'. The symbolic darkness of this act and the drive that motivates it is made clearer by other references: it is Queen Hecate, the Goddess of Night, witchcraft and evil power, as well as her nature, that Medea venerates and calls on. The source of her power, and her own nature, is something dark, primal and mysterious. By contrast, the innocence and purity of those she kills is depicted: the children are young, and 'young heads and painful thoughts don't go together'. The princess Glauce is described as having the same innocent, fair sweetness as the children, in fact, she is almost a child herself.

In Tennessee Williams <u>A Streetcar Named Desire</u>, as he himself made clear, there are no absolute villains or heroes. However, there is certainly an opposition between good and bad. Like Medea, Blanche is torn in two by different drives: on the one hand, she is the prim, ladylike girl from Belle Reve's 'white columns', and on the other, the highly sensual and rather dark seductress. Like Medea, part of her nature is tender and caring, yet when provoked, there is something dark and frightening about her. In the scene where Mitch confronts her with the truth, she compares herself to a tarantula capturing men as her victims. Later, as she threatens Stanley with the sharp glass of a broken bottle, he calls her a ' tiger'. The same dark animal instinct is in Medea's 'savage' manner, wild like a 'lioness' and a 'tiger', as the nurse describes her.

The contrast of light and dark is further used to symbolic effect in both plays to show the theme of truth and illusion. <u>Medea</u> opens with the consequences of Medea's disillusionment: wretched and miserable, she describes her husband's betrayal. He had been her 'whole life', and for many years she had done all he asked of her and more. She had worshipped him as Blanche worshipped Allan, beyond reason and beyond limits. They had both suffered cruelly on having their eyes opened to reality, although Medea arguably more as she had been deceived by Jason's very character, his nature and his promises. When Allan died, 'the searchlight that had been turned on the world was turned off again' for Blanche, and for Medea, the loss of the one she had loved more than anything, drained the meaning from her life. Medea feels she was blind to Jason before, he says he was 'mad' to ever have brought her home with him.

As a way of coping with the harsh light of reality both Blanche and Medea resort to illusion to help them survive. Medea is conscious of the deception she creates: it is all deliberate and calculated, as she 'schemes with all her skill'. A victim of Jason's deception, she now resolves to use this same ploy to her advantage. Carefully and cleverly, she deceives Creon, the Princess Glauce, Jason, and even manages to coax an oath out of Aegeus in order to complete her plan. Now that she knows the truth, she can employ illusion, and keep her enemies in the dark so as to wound them most hurtfully.

The illusion that Blanche turns to, however, is less conscious, less deliberate, and does not aim at revenge. Her world was shattered, and she does not have Medea's dark yet heroic strength. She hides from the light because she does not want others to see her as she really is. One of her first sentences to Stella is to turn the light off, as she 'won't be looked at in this merciless glare'. This persists right through the play and is particularly evident in the confrontation with Mitch, when she screams at him not to turn on the light, as 'the darkness is comforting' to her. Her avoidance of realism in favour of magic, though, is at *least as much concerning how she perceives the world as how the world perceives her. Frightened of the harsh light of reality, she prefers to cover the light with a paper lantern, to cover the plain features of the house with pretty throws, and to avoid the uncompromising light of day, hiding instead among things that are 'soft', that 'shimmer and glow'.*

Medea draws power from the dark, and thence finds courage to stand the 'light' and win her own victory, but Blanche is unable to face real light, and like a moth prefers the gentle glow of candles or artificial lights, something to illumine the darkness but not so much as to reveal everything. Medea is bold and fearless, either worshipping the night-goddess or the heat of the sun-god, her ancestor, but Blanche lives in a half-world, neither dark nor light, nothing too threatening. She must have a little 'shimmer and glow', but equally, plenty of shadow. Like Medea, Blanche deceives people into seeing her in a different light than what she really is, but she does not regard these people as fools. She has no liking for the harsh truth of reality: she tells 'what ought to be the truth', in trying to fit the world into her image of how she would like it to be. She knows that light is not always synonymous with 'good'; it is often painful and dangerous.

In <u>Medea</u> the images of light are often images of fire, and in this sense, create an impression not of pure brightness, but of something primal and powerful. Fire often is the kind of light that complements the dark, not that opposes it, like daylight. This fiery kind of light serves to echo the darkness of Medea's nature rather than to dispel it. A descendant of the sun-god, she has some ancient and dangerous power, symbolized by the objects she has received from him. This is not so much a benevolent, light-giving sun, as one that creates flames of destruction. This is the fiery rage than consumes Medea, and the literal flames that consume the princess and her father, burning and melting her enemies without mercy. This has a final echo in the last scene when Medea appears, protected by the sun-god, driven by two fire-breathing dragons, dangerous, passionate and cruel.

The light in <u>A Streetcar Named Desire</u> is not so fiery and menacing. There are the coloured lights that flicker brightly, symbolic of the relationship between Stanley and Stella, and then the shaded lights and covered lamps that Blanche enjoys. What flames there are, are gentle: the pretty candles on Blanche's birthday cake are harmless and innocent, so much so that she feels they should be saved for babies' birthdays. She wants candles to shine in babies' eyes, hoping that they will not be replaced by the cold electric light, the real enemy.

It is clear that the ever-present theme of light and dark can be repeated and re-interpreted in many ways: generally opposing one another, they can complement each other, while representing a variety of meanings. Light and dark can symbolise degrees of truth, of good, of knowledge and beauty. Most interestingly, light is not always good or darkness bad, although this is the usual association. Some of the most interesting conflicts arise when this is inverted. In any case, the effect of such a symbolic contrast is hugely effective to any audience.

Comments on the essay

This exam essay (five and a half sides of handwritten work) has many fine qualities. The candidate's knowledge of the texts is outstanding and this allows her to develop ideas to suit the question. Ideas are well supported by close reference to the text with short quotations, often single words, that are incorporated easily into the flow of the prose. She has obviously planned it carefully, as the structure is clear, moving from one text to the other to illustrate a series of ideas, rather than dealing with each text at length. This permits her to compare interestingly, to find subtle differences, and to come up with perceptive ideas and conclusions such as light not being wholly good, or fire/flames being used very differently in each text.

The question itself implicitly demands an awareness of literary features (contrasts, images, symbolism), and these are dealt with in detail, though not specifically referred to as features, along with implied awareness of further aspects. For example, there is the discussion of allusions (especially in *Medea*), of metaphors and symbols associated with objects on stage such as candles and light bulbs in *Streetcar*, and of contrasts and inner conflicts emerging in the structure of monologues. It is perhaps a pity that having mentioned the literal as well as symbolic potential of light and darkness on stage, some exploration of such stage or theatrical effects in *Streetcar* especially, is not forthcoming.

How well has she answered the question? *Streetcar* is an ideal text to use, and she has picked up most of the relevant references to light and dark. *Medea* is a less obvious choice, but she has carefully exploited the possibilities by focusing on implied darkness and using fire as a variation of light. The depiction of inner conflict of the opening paragraphs is perhaps less convincing as an example of light and dark, but she argues her case, and given the exploration of the theme in the essay as a whole, it is hardly damaging.

The language, and notably the punctuation, is both careful and effective.

Sample Two: The Novel and Short Story (Higher Level 2001)

> *Compare the uses and abuses of power as a theme in novels or short stories you have read. Say what this theme and its presentation contribute to each work you discuss.*

The use and / or abuse of power as a theme in novels cannot be discussed until we clarify what is meant by power. For the purpose of this essay, we will take power to be the capacity to exert force –either emotionally or physically, by one individual or group over another individual or group. Having defined this concept, it could be argued that in Beloved and Wuthering Heights, power is used by the authors to produce three main effects. Firstly, to produce conflict between characters who become involved in some kind of power relationship. Further, to manipulate the reader's sympathy for particular characters, and lastly to portray the complexity of human relationships. Depending on the way the author chooses to present this power – whether they show a character abusing or using their power, whether they present it symbolically or literally, a different contribution will be made to the novel.

Both Morrison and Bronte show frequent literal examples of individuals exerting their power over others, although the source of this power – or the "kind" of power – and its effects may be very different in each book. Morrison shows this in her portrayal of white dominance and cruel abuse of power held by one race over another –the product of years of social discrimination and bigotry, which holds far-reaching social and historical consequences. Her portrayal of the power white people hold in the novel shows power that stems from a society that has this imbalance of power so deeply implemented that it becomes an assumed "right", and in exercised without thought or provocation. On the other hand Bronte, describing Heathcliff's revenge, is focusing on a personal struggle for power in an isolated time and place, a calculated drive for power that stems from personal need for revenge (over Hindley at first, then later the Lintons).

To emphasize the theme of power, and to add force to the effect they wish to produce, Both Bronte and Morrison choose to explore symbolic representations of power in their novels. These primarily take the form of recurring motifs – objects that have come to symbolize one character's power or power status within a relationship. Sethe's abuse of her power as a mother is represented in the hacksaw that she uses to kill her young daughter –and the scar Beloved is left with continues the symbolic representation of this abuse of power. Power is symbolically embodied in hardware objects such as this hacksaw, the chains used to forcefully attach people in the chain gang Paul D. belongs to, and the humiliating metal collar he is forced to wear by the schoolteacher as punishment. The child's ribbon, with a piece of scalp attached, found by Stamp Paid is a further graphic and particularly powerful symbol of the cruel domination and inhumanity of the whites.

In a similar way to Beloved, locks and keys in Wuthering Heights provide physical representations of the fluctuation of power relationships between the characters. In his childhood, Heathcliff is locked away by Hindley when the Lintons came to visit, just as he is locked out of the Lintons' house when Cathy and he are caught spying. Later on, in dramatic role reversal, Heathcliff locks Cathy (the younger) and Nelly in at Wuthering Heights to prevent them going to Thrushcross Grange where Edgar is dying.

Power, although not necessarily always used to inflict pain, is exercised to gain control over other people. Obviously, this can create inequality between people – where one is the oppressed or the victim of an abuse of power, which invariably leads to conflict. Conflict appears throughout both novels – between the blacks and whites in Beloved, between Sethe and Beloved, and Beloved and Paul D., and In Wuthering Heights between Heathcliff and Linton, amongst others - all conflicts which arise from an imbalance of power in the relationship.

For Toni Morrison, there is not much difference between whether this power is expressed in the cruel and harsh ways of the schoolteacher's nephews who rape Sethe and steal her milk, or the Garners who "run a different kind of slavery" - which is still slavery. The white's perspective, appearing only once in the book – when the slave catcher and schoolteacher come to take Sethe back to Sweet Home – is undermined by their limited and crude account of the events they witness. Therefore our sympathy is directed towards the slaves who are victims of the harsh and inhuman way the whites impose their power. Heathcliff's abuse of power, however, is not seen in such an unsympathetic light, due to the fact that his drive for power is somewhat " justified" to the reader because of his harsh treatment at the hands of Hindley during his childhood. Hindley is portrayed in a much more unsympathetic light due to frequent references to him abusing his power without any motive or reason, such as when he throws his baby son over the banisters in a drunken rage, or his bullying of Heathcliff as a child.

Further, the complexity of the human relationships In Wuthering Heights is dependent on the emotional and physical power the characters exercise over each other. Heathcliff calculates his rise to financial and legal power over the Lintons, yet remains weak and a victim to the power of Catherine's love, which drives him mad. Thus, the novel operates on several levels – levels of emotional power struggles such as the love triangle including Catherine, Heathcliff and Edgar (where Catherine holds the majority of the power), as well as legal or financial matters which, by creating status differences and imbalance of power, involve the characters in complex relationships.

In the same way, Morrison uses power as a theme to create inequality between the characters in Beloved. The constant tug-of-war between love and guilt in Beloved and Sethe's relationship creates a dynamic power struggle within an intensely complex relationship. Beloved holds power over Sethe because of the intense love Sethe feels for her child –yet this love is caught up in a net of guilt, and Beloved's power increases as Sethe is drained emotionally by her child who is greedy for her, and greedy for her love. As such, Beloved becomes an incredibly powerful character in the novel, developing from a ghostly, spiteful presence at the beginning, into someone who appears to be draining Sethe of life through a constant demand for love and attention –a drive for power over the mother who killed her.

We can see that power is used as an important theme in both Beloved and Wuthering Heights, and to many similar, intended effects, yet appearing in different forms and with different consequences. Although their literary techniques may be compared, it could be said that Bronte focuses on a particular set of characters in a particular setting, and uses this theme to add complexity to her novel. Morrison uses it within a wider and more ambiguous context, to fiercely question the power any human being should hold over another – be it a mother's power over her children, or the power of one human race over another.

Comment on the sample

The length and complexity of novels, the sheer number of characters and events, creates a particular challenge when answering an exam question, and it is therefore important to establish well-defined boundaries to the discussion when dealing with this genre. This candidate does this well in the introductory paragraph, defining the keyword in the question (power) for her purposes, and drawing together two very different and intricate works in three valid and clearly defined ways. She adheres quite carefully to this argument – involving the ideas of conflict, sympathy and complexity - as she develops the essay.

The second paragraph skilfully condenses the plots and themes of these novels to a pattern illustrating the idea of power, showing her grasp of the whole text in each case and her ability to apply it to the question. She then develops (in the third paragraph) the idea of racial power and personal revenge respectively - the core of these novels - through the exploration of a literary feature – symbolic objects, concretely illustrating the idea of power through specific references.

In the second half of the essay she develops each strand of her argument in turn. Conflicts are identified, but not explored very much in terms of significance and effect. The themes of sympathy and complexity are more successfully and fully compared with persuasive examples.

In all, the candidate controls her answer well, though there is not the same density and detail of reference as in the previous drama essay, nor, perhaps the same sense of personal response. Structure and language are clear, and the candidate is notably strong on analysis, a rather rare quality.

1. Introduction

What is Internal Assessment?

It consists of two compulsory oral activities for each student:

(1) The Individual Oral Presentation (based on works in Part Four)
(2) The Individual Oral Commentary (based on works for detailed study in Part Two)

- Each is worth 15% of your final grade, 30% in total.
- Each takes a maximum of fifteen minutes.
- Both orals are assessed by your teacher, but the Oral Commentary is also externally moderated. That is to say that samples of taped orals and the teacher's marks are sent to an Examiner who will check that your teacher is applying the assessment criteria in line with standards worldwide.

The orals together are worth more marks than any other component, so you should work to ensure good performance in them.

When are the orals carried out?

Usually some time between the summer of the first year and March of the second year. Each school organizes them in a way that best suits its calendar. The Presentation and the Oral Commentary may be separated by several months, or organized close together. They may be done in class-time, but the Oral Commentary, which is taped, is usually arranged individually with the teacher. You should be given ample notice of when each activity is to take place. Sample tapes are sent to the Examiner in April of the second year.

2. The Individual Oral Commentary

Seven things you need to know about it

- It is a commentary (an organized response) based on a passage selected by your teacher of about 40 lines from one of your Part Two texts (three texts at Standard Level, four at Higher). The passage might be from a Shakespeare play, a poem by one of the poets you have studied, a passage from a novel, or a passage from a work of non-fiction.

- The commentary will be taped.

- You must be clear which texts are eligible for use.

- You should not know in advance from which Part Two text the passage will be taken.

- At the scheduled time, you will be given the passage on a photocopied sheet (no texts allowed) and will have twenty minutes to prepare your response. There should be no footnotes or Act divisions or other information on the photocopied sheet. You may take the notes you write in the preparation time into the exam room with the passage.

- The teacher is required to give you guiding questions (usually two are recommended) to help you address significant aspects. Ideally one question is on the content and one on style. You should consider these carefully. However, you do not have to answer them specifically. You may structure your response in any way you feel appropriate to the passage, provided you cover all significant elements. You should certainly not restrict yourself to the questions on your passage.

- You will normally be expected to speak for 8-12 minutes without interruption. When you have finished, your teacher is required to ask questions that will help enhance your performance. These may include points you have missed or points you made that need clarification or expansion. The teacher's role is to help you perform to the best of your ability, not to catch you out. Timing is important and you should not over-run the fifteen minutes assigned.

Five ways to help prepare for a good oral commentary

Such an oral may seem daunting, but there are a number of ways in which you can help yourself to be well prepared.

(i) The careful study of texts.

This is not an 'unseen', as in the Exam Commentary. You should have studied these works in detail in class, so it is up to you to ensure that as you study, you take careful notes. Chapter Two: How to Study Texts is designed to help you with this. Use it! The section on working with 'selected passages' is particularly applicable. The exercise is above all an examination of *detail*, how details work in the passage and how they relate to the whole.

You cannot be taught every page of your texts in minute detail, but you can learn to recognize significant passages, and acquire the technique of analysing passages closely. Thus you can address details of your passage with confidence even if you haven't specifically been taught these in class.

All the other work you do in the programme on other texts, including the writing you do, should help you with this exercise. For example, the work on written commentary for the exam is quite closely related to this especially in terms of discussion of detail, of literary features, and the finding of a structure for the response. The more effort you put into your reading and writing, the easier you will find this exercise. Also, the better your grasp of the texts and your familiarity with them, the easier you will find it to talk for the required length of time.

(ii) Recognizing literary features and appreciating their effects

You are expected to discuss literary features in your oral, so you should be familiar with both terms and features, and have given thought to the effects they can create. Chapters One, Two and Three in this guide all discuss literary features in detail, so you should read these carefully. The glossary contains a convenient list of terms.

(iii) Oral Practice

However carefully you study and write and prepare, it is true that launching into an unbroken ten to twelve-minute oral needs practice. Even one practice oral will teach you a lot about the process. Some schools give practice in oral commentary, some don't, but in either case you can improve your performance by working with a peer as follows. One plays examiner, choosing the passage and preparing to tape the session, then listens to and assesses the other. Then, or later, reverse the roles. You learn a lot by being examiner, as you need to choose and prepare the passage with care, in order to ask appropriate questions. You also learn about what is required by having to apply the assessment criteria.

You can also strengthen your oral skills by making the effort to contribute to class discussion regularly and by working with a friend or group discussing your texts. Speaking persuasively in complete, accurately constructed sentences with an appropriate vocabulary is not an art learnt at the last minute. It takes a conscious effort and practice over time.

(iv) The use of samples or models

Your teacher should be provided (from August 2003) with samples of orals on tape from the IB, together with Examiners' comments and assessment. These give a good idea of what to aim for and what to avoid. However, you may not know the texts, so if your teacher can play some tapes from candidates in previous years at your school, this could be even more helpful.

The samples provided below in this chapter, transcripts of real orals, should also help you understand what to aim at. Read them and the analyses carefully.

(v) Knowing the assessment criteria

You should ensure that your teacher provides you with a copy of these to work with. The criteria differ from those of the other components in that they add up to more marks (a total of 30). Two of the criteria (*B: Interpretation and Personal Response*; and *C: Presentation*) carry ten marks each rather than the five of all other criteria. You should pay particular attention to these and consider what it takes to perform well on them. In addition, some of the criteria only appear in this component, such as *'critical personal response'* (B) and the appropriate use of *'literary terms'* (D).

The following discussion of the criteria is based on Examiners' comments on candidate performance in the past few years, and indicates what you should focus on. The descriptors are taken from the fourth highest band out of five: the good to excellent.

3. Interpreting the assessment criteria: guidance on areas of difficulty

Criterion A: Knowledge and understanding of the content of the extract (total 5)

- *Good knowledge and understanding of the extract or work*
- *Good knowledge of the appropriate context of the extract or work*

Context is important, though the *focus* of your commentary should be on the passage. Provide the context at the beginning or near the beginning of your commentary. Different texts require different degrees of 'context'.

If you have a Shakespeare passage or an extract from a novel the context may need to be quite specific in order to show how what precedes the passage affects it, how the passage fits into the sequence of the work, and perhaps, what the consequences are. This is why you need to know the sequence of your works clearly. Avoid vagueness such as: "This comes somewhere in the second half of the play". Also, remember that in a play other characters may be present on stage at this point who are not referred to in the passage itself, but may need to be mentioned.

Sample section of an oral commentary showing context

For example, let us suppose that you were given Macbeth's soliloquy about Banquo from Act Three. You might briefly introduce the passage and its focus, and then say:

> *This soliloquy takes place near the beginning of Act Three shortly after Macbeth has murdered Duncan and been crowned King. The scene is in fact the first time we see Macbeth since the night of the murder, and this soliloquy is the first indication we have of his state of mind, which is full of doubt about Banquo.*
>
> *The speech has a particular edge to it because we have just heard Banquo in soliloquy expressing his intuition about Macbeth's 'foul play', and referring to the witches' prophecy that he, Banquo, would be the father of kings.*
>
> *There's also a kind of irony because Macbeth and Banquo have just had a dialogue about the 'great feast' tonight where Banquo is to be the chief guest and Macbeth appears to be flattering him and relying on him.*
>
> *The speech in the passage is framed by Macbeth asking his servant confidentially for some 'men' he seems to have engaged, who enter immediately after the speech and are hired to murder Banquo. Of course we don't know that until after the speech but there's a certain mood of fear and insecurity as the speech begins. The implications of the soliloquy become clearer afterwards when we find out that Macbeth is already planning Banquo's death.*

This is quite an elaborate contextualisation (and yes, such precision is rare), but you can see how the understanding of the extract is enhanced by it and how it is all relevant to the passage. It only takes about half a minute, leaving plenty of time for discussion of the passage.

Shakespeare plays lend themselves to sharp placing of the passage, but other texts may work differently.

If you are given a poem, the contextualising would not be like the above. It might be appropriate to say something of the circumstances of the poem, or to place it in the body of the poet's work. You should certainly at some point or at different points in the commentary make links between the poem and other poems you have read by the same poet or another poet in your study (referring to thematic concerns or devices, or contrasting attitudes, for example in war poets). A poem should not be treated as a separate entity, just as the Shakespeare passage needs to be seen in the wider context of the play.

However, the references you make must be relevant, *enriching your points about the poem provided.* A Robert Frost poem expressing an attitude to death should not be a springboard for a lengthy discussion of death in Emily Dickinson and John Donne. Learnt chunks of biography tend to be annoying rather than impressive; succinct and relevant links are appreciated.

Criterion B. Interpretation and personal response (total 10)

- *A generally valid interpretation of the thought and feeling expressed in the extract, including some degree of personal response*
- *Clear awareness and some analysis of the effects of literary features*
- *The response is supported by relevant references to the extract*

It is not for nothing that this criterion carries so many marks. It is concerned with an engaged, individual, personal perspective. It should show that you have gone beyond a dutiful noting of what your teacher has said, or what you have read, and that you have 'internalised' ideas and opinions and thought for yourself. How do you get to that point? Many of the approaches outlined below and elsewhere in this guide should help, especially Chapter Two: How to Read Texts'. The samples provided later in this chapter should demonstrate the individual perspective.

'Thought and feeling'

The first two bulleted points often present difficulties. 'Thought and feeling' can be tough challenges especially in Shakespeare and poetry where the text can be ambiguous and complex. It is one thing to *explain* and *comment on* what is being said, but another to enter into the character's mind and suggest what he/she is feeling. This often requires some intuition and imagination, in addition to intelligence. But if you don't do it, response will be hard, because 'response' tends to involve emotion or understanding of emotion. For example, in Banquo's brief soliloquy before the scene with Macbeth, described above, he says:

> Thou hast it now: King, Cawdor, Glamis, all,
> As the weird sisters promised, and I fear
> Thou play'dst most foully for it; yet it was said
> It should not stand in thy posterity,
> But that myself should be the root and father
> Of many kings....

Typically, a candidate will explain that Banquo is here referring to the witches' utterances delivered to Macbeth when he is riding back from battle with Banquo near the beginning of the play (though the three titles were promised to him in reverse order from those here). The candidate might go on to explain that at the time, Banquo had reservations about listening to the 'sisters', but Macbeth was susceptible to the prophecies, and so on.

It is less typical for candidates to explore why Banquo may be saying this and in what frame of mind. Is he morally judgmental, or detached about the foul play? Is he meditating, or alarmed by the possibility? Is he secretly ambitious, attracted by the idea of being the father of kings, or simply pondering what the witches said? What might he be thinking and feeling, and why? There is no certainty, but you can suggest possibilities and alternatives, backed up by references to the text.

Any actor would have to make his mind up about what he was feeling and why before he uttered the lines, and it often helps to put yourself in the position of the actor (or the narrator of a poem). The meaning of plays often lies in the way they are spoken and heard. Listening to a good cassette recording of a play, or watching a good stage or film version, can help a lot to suggest thoughts and emotions, and it is a good idea to revise with one of these. Similarly poetry and novel recordings can be enlightening.

'Literary features'

These often present another difficulty, especially with Shakespeare. Candidates are often insufficiently aware of what these 'features' are. They can cope with the odd simile or metaphor, but more rarely recognize structure, syntax, punctuation and other effects. The sections on literary features in Chapters One, Two, and Three of this guide are designed to make these clearer to you. Read them!

The candidate quoted above in the 'context' sample is responding to a dramatic or theatrical effect. She appreciates the effect of the Macbeth's furtive command to bring in the 'men', right before his soliloquy, as it increases the suspense and fear in the atmosphere. This certainly counts as a literary feature. We can see here how her appreciation of this is part of a response to the whole, not just a 'feature' identified or listed. Staging effects, mood, sounds, etc., can all be referred to when relevant.

In prose non fiction, fiction and poetry, the narrator and the 'voice' are very important as a feature or part of the artifice. To help prepare you to recognize these more easily and to remind you of the variety of possibilities, you should study the 'checklists' on prose and poetry in Chapter One: Commentary, and the list of approaches to non-fiction later in this chapter.

Sometimes teachers provide a shortlist of features to use in the commentary, but there can be a danger here. Each passage has its own set of features. You should begin by looking for what is distinctive about the passage, rather than applying a list artificially. In other words, you should work from the inside outwards.

Criterion C. Presentation (total 10)

- *Clear and logical structure to the response*
- *The response is focused and presented in a clear, coherent, effectiv, and convincing manner*
- *Supporting references to the passage, where relevant, are appropriately integrated into the body of the response*

As you see, this criterion also carries a lot of marks. It is the heart of the 'oral' aspect – the way you put your material across, which involves both content *and manner*. It is concerned with the way you organize your material, and with the way you present it orally. Although it does not specifically say so, this includes how it *sounds*. It cannot be effective and convincing if it is dreary, slow and monotonous. It is more likely to if it sounds engaged and interested. You are performing for an audience. The more involvement you have with your material (along, of course, with understanding), the more likely it is that you will be persuasive.

Structure

This is one of the main weaknesses in performance in this exercise. How can one learn to do it well? There is no single way to structure a commentary, no one formula that works for all passages. Through practice, you can develop a feel for the focus of an extract, and its significant elements. To some extent, this sense of focus will be personal, just as ten students writing on the same text will respond to the same material slightly differently.

One strategy is:

(i) Read through the passage attentively and decide what the main interest or significance is. In the case of drama or prose where the passage is part of a wider whole, this might be a turning point in the plot or narrative, a shift in the relationship of characters, or an illustration of a central symbol or issue. To establish this focus and keep it in mind throughout the oral is very important.

(ii) Look at the shape of the passage itself. Is there a distinctive movement in it, towards a climax or change, or towards one point and then in another direction? Does it fall into several clear sections? If so, how do these relate or link? Are there tensions or oppositions or contrasts? Between what or whom?

(iii) Work through the passage listing all the elements and features you would want to include in your discussion. This might include images and language features, references that need explaining, character traits, etc.

(iv) Decide how your main ideas might best be grouped in, say, three main ways, and how the details might relate to these.

Samples of structures

If you look at the extract from the opening of *Pride and Prejudice* in Chapter Two: How to Study Texts (p.37-38), you can see how to arrive at a structure, though you might want to organize the points differently. For example, you might say, having established context and provided a summarizing statement of what the passage is about:

I would like to discuss the effectiveness of the passage as an opening and how it illustrates some of Jane Austen's narrative techniques, with a focus on the narrative voice and dialogue. I would also like to discuss the characters of Mr and Mrs Bennet and the theme of marriage.

You would then have established a direction for your commentary and can ensure that all your main ideas will be covered. There is nothing wrong with proceeding in a more or less linear way *provided you have established a clear direction*. Think of it like the introduction to a World Literature assignment or an Exam Essay where *the clear line of approach needs to be established in the introduction*.

What you want to avoid is starting with the first line or sentence of the passage or poem and merely plodding through giving a kind of paraphrase (re-stating the content in your own words), making points in a random and unconnected way (*'At the beginning we see...and then.. and then..'*).

If you know your texts well, establishing a structure will not be too difficult. You can practise by taking passages, perhaps working with a friend, and develop the skill of identifying focus, coherence, and significant elements. The 'chapter notes organised in headings' approach as you study (described in Chapter Two: How to Study Texts) is a very helpful preparation.

With poetry it is often necessary to move in a linear way because the development of thought is usually tightly structured, but you should still establish at the outset the focus and impact of the work and the main features that you want to cover. For example, if you were given Wilfred Owen's "Dulce Et Decorum Est", reproduced below, you might say:

In discussing the poem I particularly want to focus on Owen's use of diction, his sound effects and his tone.

You do not have to then discuss these three elements in 'chunks', one after another, but in following the logic of the poem's development, you can keep referring to these elements, amongst others, and they will help give a focus and shape to your commentary.

Obviously you cannot control your performance as you can a written essay, even if you have a plan. In an oral, you are not expected to. You should not try in your preparation time to write out whole sentences and paragraphs that you then read out in the exam room. That is not an 'oral'. Ideas may come to you as you go along and it is fine for you to voice these if they relate to your scheme. Similarly, the spontaneity of your answers or responses to your teacher's questions is a different thing from your prepared commentary, and can reflect another strength.

Criterion D: Use of Language (total 5)

- **The language is clear, varied, precise, appropriate**
- **No significant lapses in grammar and expression**

- **Suitable choice of register and style**
- **Some literary terms used appropriately**

For the highest level of performance (5) the choice of register should be 'effective', use of vocabulary 'wide', and grammatical structures 'varied'.

Although your style cannot be as formal and concise as a written essay might be, this is a formal exercise and requires a careful choice of vocabulary and attention to sentence structure. Avoid the colloquial ('Hamlet's Dad', 'good guys', 'goofy') and casual imprecision ('kind of, you know'). It is hard to launch into a sentence without knowing exactly how you are going to formulate it, and the formation of complete and correct sentences in such an oral is a challenge. Practice helps.

You probably know your own speech tendencies and can begin to eliminate bad habits. If you tape an oral with a friend you can listen carefully to your speech and think of ways to improve it. Attentive reading and writing should help improve your oral performance, too.

'Register' (a popular word in the criteria) means the form of language appropriate to the occasion, in this case, 'formal' rather than 'informal'.

How can I be sure to speak for that long?

Students are often afraid they won't be able to do this, and indeed quite a number only manage six or seven minutes. But this is usually because they don't know the work well enough to have much to say. If you have studied well and become involved with the text, you probably won't find it difficult to speak for ten minutes. Knowing the text well is arguably the single most important factor in good performance. Another is having a strategy, as outlined above and elsewhere in this guide, so that your plan gives you a good basis for discussion.

4. Non-fiction texts: how to approach them for successful performance

Non-fiction texts can be very interesting to read, but how to discuss them analytically and effectively may not be so evident. They may not appear to contain the same kind of density of literary interest as a poem or a passage from Shakespeare or Hardy. However, you can attain the same kind of excellence in performance on a non-fiction passage as on any other.

Appropriate ways of approaching your non-fiction text depend to some extent on the kind of non-fiction it is: essays or autobiography, for example. If it is essays you may need to consider content. What is the thesis of a particular essay? Does this rest on assumptions, with which you may or may not agree, facts, or opinions. How compellingly are these put across? By what means: anecdote, contrast, facts, or other techniques? If on the other hand you are dealing with an autobiography that extends over a long period of time, you may need to think, as with a novel, more about the relation of part to whole, about things like the selection of materials, the degree of personal involvement in different sections, the voice, etc. Any passage will call for comparison and links with other parts of the work.

The following list may help shape your responses to non-fiction

- For what kind of audience does it seem to be intended? What suggests that?
- What context drives the material: the personal, cultural, social, historic, other?
- What seems to be the purpose or intention of the writer? To persuade, educate or inform, appeal to the emotions or senses, to share...?
- How involved does the writer seem in his/her material?
- What is the writer or narrator's perspective: an older reflective self, a central player, a witness?
- What impression do we gain of this narrator? What conveys that impression?
- What tone predominates? Anger, nostalgia, bitterness? Does the tone vary?

- How is the work structured? Are there patterns or parallels? What effects does that structure produce?
- What is the predominant method of development: argument, narrative, description, examples?
- Is there anything striking about the style: sentence or paragraph structure, or punctuation?
- Does the writer use much imagery? What effects are achieved by it?
- Are figures of speech (metaphors, alliteration, etc.) or other literary features used? What effects are created?
- If a diary, does it seem intended for an audience? How conscious does the style seem?
- What do you most respond to in this writing? What helps create that response?

5. Some samples of individual oral commentaries

Sample One (Standard Level) Shakespeare: *Macbeth*

Read the following passage and decide on the most important elements to discuss. Think about how these might best be structured.

Macbeth:

> To be thus is nothing,
> But to be safely thus. Our fears in Banquo
> Stick deep, and in his royalty of nature
> Reigns that which would be feared. 'Tis much he dares,
> And to that dauntless temper of his mind
> He hath a wisdom that doth guide his valour
> To act in safety. There is none but he
> Whose being I do fear; and under him
> My genius is rebuked, as it is said
> Mark Anthony's was by Caesar. He chid the sisters,
> When first they put the name of king upon me
> And bade them speak to him. Then, prophet-like,
> They hailed him father to a line of kings.
> Upon my head they placed a fruitless crown,
> And put a barren sceptre in my gripe,
> Thence to be wrenched with an unlineal hand,
> No son of mine succeeding. If it be so,
> For Banquo's issue have I filed my mind,
> For them the gracious Duncan have I murdered,
> Put rancours in the vessel of my peace
> Only for them, and mine eternal jewel
> Given to the common enemy of man,
> To make them kings, the seed of Banquo kings.
> Rather than so, come fate, into the list,
> And champion me unto the utterance.

Guiding questions:

(1) What does this extract reveal about the development of Macbeth?
(1) What linguistic means does Shakespeare use to make his development clear?

The candidate's commentary transcribed verbatim from the tape recording:

Remember that certain qualities of an oral, like the expressiveness, fluency, pace and persuasiveness of effect, cannot be conveyed in a transcript. Nor can the written transcript be judged like an essay. It is a spontaneous utterance (based only on the preparation notes), and it cannot have the same formal precision and structure of an essay.

"This particular part of the text occurs around the middle of the play after Macbeth has murdered Duncan and has taken his place as King, although we see some insecurity here. Macbeth feels threatened by Banquo's presence.

This particular part, where he says: "To be thus is nothing/ But to be safely thus", up to the last line, is Macbeth's third soliloquy. Now we see Macbeth draw a comparison between himself and Banquo. Now this has existed from near the beginning of the play. Although in the beginning they seemed quite similar, because they fought together side by side, they were victors in battle, they fought for King Duncan, they were portrayed as being noble and brave and valiant and they were praised by the King – but that's as far as the similarities go because from then on we see some clear distinctions between them.

First of all they meet the weird sisters together and they have very different reactions: Banquo questions their existence while Macbeth believes straight away what he's told, and we see he's overcome by his ambition, which Banquo isn't – he goes for logic. Also we see they're praised by Duncan and we see their different reactions. Banquo's words are measured and seem true and correct, while Macbeth's are hypocritical and sound false.

So it's obvious that Macbeth feels, as he says here, that his "genius is rebuked, as it is said/ Mark Anthony's was by Caesar". The simile Shakespeare uses here goes to show exactly the feelings Macbeth has for Banquo and it is justifed because of all we have seen in the play above. And of course he goes on to mention the different prophecies of the weird sisters, like Banquo was hailed father to a line of kings, and it's interesting here to note that Shakespeare uses alliteration like 'hailed him". It's onomatopoeic – it echoes like a stadium full of people, hailing and shouting loudly all this noise. It goes to emphasise the effect of this phrase

Macbeth on the other hand has been named King but has been given "a barren sceptre in my gripe/ thence to be wrenched with an unlineal hand/ no son of mine succeeding". Also "upon my head they placed a fruitless crown". All these are metaphors which Shakespeare uses – er – metaphors concerning the elements which are associated with the King, like sceptre and crown. "Unlineal hand" refers to the succession of kings. By the use of these metaphors Shakespeare is trying to emphasise the contrast between Banquo and Macbeth, and this is used to justify the final phrase of Macbeth and the conclusion he reaches, that " Come fate into the list/ and champion me unto the utterance." So at the end of the soliloquy Macbeth decides to kill Banquo.

One should also notice that other images and metaphors that Shakespeare creates here. He says "mine eternal jewel/ Given to the common enemy of man", which I think is a very beautiful image, because Shakespeare compares the soul of a human being to a jewel which should not be traded for anything, but Macbeth has done this for the sake of power, and to be named King, because of his ambition. And "The common enemy of man" is of course Satan, and we may note that at the end of the play the only person who stays with Macbeth is his servant Seton, whose name is pronounced Satan. Though it's not written that way, it's heard that way. So we see how Macbeth has crossed the line and has put himself away from nobility and valour and gone with all this evil. Throughout the play we see the contrast between good and evil that is presented by different characters. So Macbeth is saying here that if he lets Banquo live, it's been in vain, because he'll be overthrown again.

I get the feeling that this is a cycle because he says in his earlier, first soliloquy he was afraid that exactly this could happen, what is happening here, that after one murder (the murder of Duncan) he would be forced to proceed to do more murders, as of course we see he does, he proceeds to do atrocities. And though it began from ambition, at the end of the play he is pronounced to be a "dead butcher", and this has to do with the development of Macbeth that we see throughout the play, although we could say perhaps that the play moves in a cycle because we see that at the end of the play he is somewhat restored in our eyes. However we see that he began from the position where he didn't want to kill Duncan, and Lady Macbeth said "you are too full of the milk of human kindness", and now he has come to the point where he calls Fate to champion him to kill Banquo. And this is reminiscent of his invocation to Night, "Come sealing night", that he makes in his second soliloquy before he kills Duncan. So all the elements of Nature help Macbeth to do the murders.

It is interesting that he calls on Fate. I find it quite bizarre because there's this big question whether Macbeth is a free agent or not. Is it Fate that says that Banquo has to be murdered? He makes it sound as if he does it, justified by Fate, who says it must be this way, which of course we know is not the case because it was his choice to proceed with a murder or not. But we see here that he considers it something that can be justified because of the presence of the weird sisters, because they have named him King.

Now as a conclusion I'd like to say that we'll see further development in the play. This is only the middle, though the action, the plot, happens very quickly. We will see that he'll kill Lady Macduff for no reason, and her sons, saying that "the firstlings of my heart shall be the firstlings of my hand", or something of the sort. So this is a step in that development.

Teacher's question: I'd like to ask you – throughout the play Banquo seems to be a sort of foil to Macbeth. What sort of picture does Shakespeare paint of Banquo in this soliloquy? Do you think it's an accurate one?

Candidate's response: Well, not very, because Macbeth said he (Banquo) "chid the sisters /when first they put the name of king upon me", and we know that's not true, because Banquo didn't interfere at all, he didn't want to listen for himself, for his own fate. He didn't show "vaulting ambition" that Macbeth says of himself that he has. In my opinion it's as if Macbeth is trying to find reasons to kill him, as if he's trying to persuade himself that this is the right thing to do, as we have seen him do before in his previous soliloquies where he's trying to persuade himself to kill Duncan, and at first he reaches the conclusion that no, because he (Duncan) is a kinsman, because he's King, his guest, and he cannot proceed to do this. Then of course Lady Macbeth interferes, and, er, he makes up the reasons that justify this killing, and this is Fate, because the witches have told him he'll be king. So he thinks this gives him the right to murder. And of course it's noticeable here that Lady Macbeth doesn't interfere any more at all –she has no knowledge of the murder of Banquo, not until after it has occurred. And a little after this speech he tell Lady Macbeth, "Be innocent of the knowledge, dearest chuck".

Teacher: Yes, he's acting completely alone at this point – you're right. One final question: Towards the end of the soliloquy he repeats the phrase –"for them", "for them". Would you like to comment on the effect of the repetition of these words?

Candidate: Well, by the actual word I think he means Banquo's children who will be succeeding him, like Fleance whom they don't manage to kill because he escapes. I think the constant repetition shows some contempt in the way it is said, as if he's despising them, looking down on them, perhaps as if he doesn't think they should be kings –and of course it- the repetition- shows the contrast of Macbeth and them. It emphasises the clear distinction between the two parts.

Teacher: That's right. Thank you very much. This is the end of the recording

Comment on the sample

Overall comment: The candidate is in firm control of her material, which gives the commentary a clear direction, fluency and persuasiveness (more apparent in the taped version). There is hardly a pause or hesitation in the initial unbroken ten-minute presentation. That fluency is especially marked in the unusually long sentences, which she carries through grammatically, driven by her sound grasp of the text. The oral seems to be a genuine communication. Sentences, especially at the beginning, are not prepared and read like an essay, as is sometimes the case with candidates, nor is there any sense that she is regurgitating ideas learnt in class. There is a spontaneity about the whole oral.

The performance in relation to the assessment criteria: The candidate does not discuss the immediate context in great detail. (The example showing context on this passage earlier in this chapter reveals how much is gained by a sharp awareness of what frames the passage.) However, she has an good sense of the passage in relation to the wider context and structure of the whole play, especially Macbeth's psychological development. She shows ease in referring closely to earlier and later parts of the play relevant to the given passage (this is particularly important when dealing with passages from plays and novels or long works). Though she does not announce the structure she will follow, there is an implicit order to the oral. She avoids a plodding line-by-line explanation, instead, covering significant elements and sections in the passage sequentially.

She moves from a comparison of Banquo and Macbeth's characters relevant to the first part of the passage, to an explanation of the metaphorical language of the central part, which indicates a 'justification' for the killing. In following the movement of thought, she also deals with the specifics of language, the meaning of metaphors and allusions – "lineal", "jewel", "common enemy", etc. She then moves to psychological considerations, relevant to a soliloquy, showing how the passage echoes previous moments where Macbeth calls for the help of external forces. The candidate at this point shows a capacity for exploration of ideas, as she speculates on the role of Fate and free will. She concludes with a reminder about the place of the passage in the overall structure of the play.

The candidate expresses herself effectively throughout, maintaining a good level of vocabulary, relating her observations to the text through quotation, and is able to comment on the effectiveness of literary features. The follow-up questions demonstrate why these are important. They pick up on some elements in the passage that have not specifically been dealt with. The candidate is able to think on her feet and respond in some detail, though she does not deal clearly with the character of Banquo as revealed by Macbeth.

A good oral is neither exhaustive nor perfect. There may be omissions and even some errors, but in relation to the assessment criteria this candidate has reached a good level.

Sample Two (Higher Level) Poetry: "Dulce Et Decorum Est" by Wilfred Owen

As the following poem is very well known, you may want to give yourself practice by deciding how you would plan a commentary on it, and then compare with the sample provided.

Bent double, like old beggars under sacks,
Knock-kneed, coughing like hags, we cursed through sludge,
Till on the haunting flares we turned our backs
And towards our distant rest began to trudge.
Men marched asleep. Many had lost their boots
But limped on, blood-shod. All went lame; all blind;
Drunk with fatigue; deaf even to the hoots
Of tired, outstripped Five-Nines that dropped behind.

Gas! GAS! Quick, boys! – An ecstasy of fumbling,
Fitting the clumsy helmets just in time;
But someone still was yelling out and stumbling,
And flound'ring like a man in fire or lime...
Dim through the misty panes and thick green light,
As under a green sea, I saw him drowning.

In all my dreams, before my helpless sight,
He plunges at me, guttering, choking, drowning.

If in some smothering dreams you too could pace
Behind the wagon that we flung him in,
And watch the white eyes writhing in his face,
His hanging face, like a devil's sick of sin;
If you could hear, at every jolt, the blood
Come gargling from the froth-corrupted lungs,
Obscene as cancer, bitter as the cud
Of vile, incurable sores on innocent tongues,-
My friend, you would not tell with such high zest
To children ardent for some desperate glory,
The old Lie: *Dulce et decorum est*
Pro patria mori.

The candidate's commentary transcribed verbatim from the tape recording:

This poem was written in 1917 while Owen was receiving treatment at Craiglockhart hospital for shell shock. It's very typical of Owen's works because it derives from his own personal experience of the war. Firstly "Dulce et Decorum Est" is the title of the poem. It's an allusion to Horace's Odes and it means "It is sweet and fitting to die for your country."

I'm going to start with the first stanza: *"Bent double, like old beggars under sacks,*
Knock-kneed, coughing like hags, we cursed through sludge,
Till the haunting flares we turned our backs
And towards our distant rest began to trudge "

The first stanza deals mainly with the physical condition of the soldiers and it's very, he uses words like "beggars" and "hags" to show the dehumanizing condition these soldiers are in. This is like the youth of England, and they've been reduced to "hags" and "beggars", and they're limping and trudging. He uses onomatapoeia here with "sludge" and "trudge", which really emphasises the difficulty and the heaviness and fatigue that they're experiencing. And the "haunting flares" – later on in the poem we're told that he suffers from haunting nightmares and so this is sort of, this is echoed later on in the poem. Then, when he mentions "our distant rest", "towards our distant rest began to trudge", the distant rest could also be seen as the final rest, death, and sort of, the inevitability of it.

Then it continues, in the second part of the first stanza:
"Men marched asleep. Many had lost their boots
But limped on bloodshod. All went lame; all blind;
Drunk with fatigue; deaf even to the hoots
Of tired outstripped Five-Nines that dropped behind".

"Men marched asleep" is an oxymoron – because, obviously, if you're asleep you can't be marching, and just again reiterates the exhaustion that these men are experiencing. They "limped on, blood-shod". The word "shod" usually refers to horses, horses are shod, and so it's again, it's dehumanising, like degrading the soldiers to animals, almost. "All went lame; all blind". This is reminiscent of a biblical scene, and Owen was known to use a lot of biblical allusions and, er, references in his poetry because it was one of his great influences. Er, "drunk with fatigue". You think "drunk" is very incapacitated, and its sort of that they're overwhelmed and enveloped in this sort of drunk, heavy exhaustion so that they can hardly walk. And they're deaf "even to the hoots/Of tired outstripped Five-Nines that dropped behind". They're deaf even to the sound of the shells and even the shells themselves are characterised as tired, so its like the whole, the whole atmosphere is one of heavy exhaustion.

And, we have an example of internal rhyme here, "outstripped" and "dropped" and "Five Nines" and behind", and this sort of lulls, makes the last line of the stanza very lulling, with a sharp contrast with the beginning of the second stanza, which is an immediate change in pace, it's more rapid, using punctuation and capitalization. It starts: "Gas! GAS! Quick boys! –an ecstasy of fumbling,/ Fitting the clumsy helmets just in time". And its Owen going back and reliving a moment and the, the change in pace with "Gas! GAS!, Quick, boys", it really brings you back into the panic and brings you into the moment, and "an ecstasy of fumbling", you can just feel the total confusion of, er the moment.

"But someone still was yelling out and stumbling, / And flound'ring like a man in fire or lime.../ Dim, through the misty panes and thick green light,/As under a green sea, I saw him drowning". This actually is based on a true event that Owen experienced, that when they were, they were out in... a field or whatever, and there was a gas attack, and someone didn't have time to put their helmet on, and ended up dying in front of him, and it was something that really left a great impact on him, and he still dreams about it and it haunts his, his nightmares.

The use of the word "floundering" is found also used in "The Sentry" and he liked the sound of it because it really showed like the confusion and fumbling and er, the sort of helplessness of this man. He mentions the "misty panes". The panes of the gas mask were actually made of celluloid, and they would be tinted slightly green, and also the colour of the gas is like a mustardy-green colour. And he uses water imagery here, "as under a green sea I saw him drowning" to show how the gas sort of envelops you and surrounds you as if you were under water. And also "drowning", the effect of the gas on the lungs, it brings water on the lungs, and it would be the same physical effect as if you were drowning. And it really helps give the reader a vivid image of this man dying, suffering, the fact that he's drowning, he's totally helpless.

And then the next sentence or stanza –it's a one-sentence stanza:
"In all my dreams, before my helpless sight,
He plunges at me, guttering, choking, drowning".

Again we have drowning brought up again, and the use of the words "guttering, choking drowning", the repetition of sort of, like very, words that really get to you like throat- punching words that can make you really feel and imagine the suffering of this man. And the fact that this man is "plunging" at him, you can imagine in a nightmare this haunting figure coming at you, and like you, can hardly escape it. And also, "my helpless sight": it's again, it's the feeling of inability to help someone in his weakness, and also his guilt.

Then the last stanza is where the real message of his poem lies, and it starts:
"If in some smothering dreams you too could pace
Behind the wagon that we flung him in,
And watch the white eyes writhing in his face,
His hanging face, like a devil's sick of sin..."

Again, you have the smothering dreams. They're almost inescapable and you can't do anything about them. And the fact that the pronoun changes to ' you' – it's sort of shocking, because suddenly Owen's addressing the reader and as we see later, it's more society at large, it's the collective responsibility of society to take responsibility for the effect of war on these people, and the consequences.

He mentions "the wagon that we flung him in", and this is sort of paralleled with "The Sentry" because the body is no longer personal, it no longer has an identity, it's just "flung". "Flung is a really careless, inhuman word. You don't fling people, you carefully lay them, but in this case he uses the word "flung" to show how the body is no longer, is void of identity. And it's paralleled in "The Sentry" because in "The Sentry" he refers to the body as 'it' –"he dredged it up for dead", and it's dehumanising again. Also it could be paralleled with Hamlet because " the hand of little employment has the daintier sense". It's just saying that those people who are not exposed to death and war would be more shocked by the fact that this man has died and that you have to deal with the body, but these soldiers have it seen it so much, they've been basically so saturated by it that they can fling the body almost carelessly because it's something they have learnt to accept, because they've been exposed to it so much.

 And in this stanza Owen goes through the senses, you can hear, you can feel the smothering dreams and you can see, you can watch the white eyes writhing in his face - this just shows the overall impact of the whole experience, the entirety of the experience on Owen. And he continues "the Devil sick of sin". It's as if he's been saturated by the evil of it, and even a devil would be sick and could not endure as much of the evil and sin that war has created. And he continues:
"If you could hear at every jolt the blood
Come gargling from the froth-corrupted lungs,
Obscene as cancer, bitter as the cud
Of vile incurable sores on innocent tongues …"

Again, you can hear the blood gargling in the lungs and "the froth-corrupted" – it's also the physical condition that the water and liquid that would be in the lungs is frothy, but the fact that he uses "corrupted", it's almost like a moral statement and it's placed in contrast with the "innocent tongues", it's the corruption of the innocent and it sort of echoes what Owen is trying to say through the poem, that these innocent people have been exposed to such ghastly horrors that it's completely unacceptable. Also he uses the comparison of "obscene as cancer" and cancer is paralleled with war: because both spread, and grow, destroy and kill. I think It's very interesting that he chooses to use "cancer". Also, "bitter as the cud": this is paralleled with "Anthem for Doomed Youth" because the first line is "Who are these dying like cattle?", and the cud is what cows like chew up, and it parallels with animals again.

And then the last line of the poem is the punch line, the very important line. He says:
" My friend, you would not tell with such high zest
To children ardent for some desperate glory,
The old lie: Dulce Et Decorum Est
Pro patria mori",

and this is the punch line, the message that Owen was trying to get across. "My friend" is referring to Jessie Pope, who was a journalist at the time, who wrote a series of patriotic poems and basically in general he's condemning those er, those people who encourage young men to go off and fight and encourage the propaganda and the recruiting, when they themselves have not experienced the true horrors of war. And the fact that he uses the words 'children' and earlier in the poem "boys", it shows these are not men; these people are not people who have lived a long time and lived a life. These are young, the youth of England going off and being totally slaughtered and it has a deeper effect on the reader to realize that these are children who are being killed, these are not grown men.

Also the overall message of the poem is the condemnation of these people who encourage it, as well as the futility of war as a whole. An example of someone he would probably be referring to through this poem is Rupert Brooke who also wrote a series of patriotic poems, and he said in one of his poems: *"If I should die, think only this of me/ That there's some corner of a foreign field/ that is forever England"*, and Owen, coming out of the experience of it feels very bitter and resentful, and probably frustrated because he knows what war is really like, and these people back home in England don't know how horrible and terrifying the war is. The poem is very typical of Owen. As he once said: *"My subject is war and the pity of war"*, and "All a poet can do today is warn, that's why the true poets must be truthful". And it's very typical because it comes from his personal experience and because he is warning future generations, and also calling upon his own generation to take responsibility for the consequences. It's an example of how Owen really found his voice during the war.

Teacher: *Thank you very much*

Comment on the sample

This candidate shows a number of strengths. She shows a good understanding of Owen's purpose and emotions; a strong response to the content, entering imaginatively into the life of the poem, of the experience depicted; and a good appreciation of the many different effects of language. It is particularly rare for a candidate to interpret the poem, as it were, from the point of view of the poet himself, showing sympathetic and intelligent understanding of his experience. She shows insight into the connotations of words like "drunk" and "flung", and does some nice cross-referencing, showing links between words that echo or contrast with one another in different parts of the poem, such as "children" and "boys", or "haunting". Her comment on the "tired" Five-Nines is pleasing.

It is also an unhesitating performance. There may be slight adjustments and re-phrasings in mid-sentence, but as a whole the oral has a strong and compelling movement to it, indicating that she is in control of her material, that she understands both whole and parts. One senses that she both reproduces ideas and information gained in class (and this is as it should be), but goes further, reflecting her own individual, personal response and grasp (and this is what examiners would like to see more of).

Her strategy is to take the poem section by section and comment on it. This is an acceptable way to approach a poem that requires much detailed comment (the poetic techniques and effects of language are very concentrated). Also, the poem moves in a narrative and dramatic sequence, so that it makes sense to treat this sequentially. The technique of taking a few lines at a time also means that she can comment in some depth, at the same time referring to other parts of the poem where relevant.

It is very difficult to give a perfect performance, and apart from occasional lapses in vocabulary and some difficulties in following through sentences, this candidate misses something very important to this particular poem –the irony of the title and quotation that frames the poem. There is nothing "sweet or right" about such an experience, and it is a powerful use of a quotation, especially repeating it at the end. This is something that a teacher might ask in a follow-up question. While there is an implicit structure to the performance, following the narrative in a linear way, it might also have strengthened it to call attention to some striking aspects of the poem that she would address in the course of the oral: for example, diction, sound effects, and tone. This might have sharpened the structure of the presentation and facilitated links between one part and another.

6. The Individual Oral Presentation

What it is

This 10-15 minute presentation, worth 15% of your total grade, is based on a work or works in Part Four of your programme (School's Own Choice). You choose the topic (as you do with World Literature), which should reflect your personal interest in one or more of these works. You should consult your teacher about your choice of topic, to ensure that it is appropriate and will meet the criteria. You prepare the presentation in your own time. Some examples of presentations are given below.

When and how it is done

Your teacher should give you plenty of advance warning about when the presentations are to take place. They are often done towards the end of the first year, or in the first part of the second year (March would be the latest point). They may be performed in front of the class, or take place as a one-to-one experience with your teacher, as the oral commentaries usually do. The presentation may partly involve the class, for example, through questions after the presentation. Whichever way you do it, the teacher should ask you some questions at the end of the presentation, as with the oral commentary, to probe your knowledge and understanding further.

How it is marked

It is assessed only by your teacher, not by an Examiner, and does not have to be taped, though your teacher may choose to do this. However, the marks are entered on a form together with the marks for the oral commentary, and samples of these forms, together with tapes of the commentary, *are* sent to an Examiner. S/he will check that the marking is consistent.

The assessment criteria for the presentation are exactly the same as for the individual commentary. They are discussed on previous pages in this chapter, and the same comments apply. For example, you cannot be persuasive if you are largely reading your presentation, so you should take care to engage your audience. Know your material well and only use brief notes or headings. Remember, whatever you choose to do, however creative it is, it needs to reflect your knowledge and understanding of the texts and its features, and to be effectively structured and expressed. Look through the criteria and decide whether your ideas can meet these.

The advantage of freedom of choice

This is one of the few areas in the A1 programme where you can really follow your own interests, both intellectual and creative, in a way that you choose. You can bring in your own talents, such as debating, writing, acting, art or music, as you see from some of the examples below. You can be a little experimental and exploratory, and should enjoy the opportunity. You also control the quality of your performance in that you have plenty of time to prepare and practice, and can make it as effective as possible.

Choice of topic may include:

- ***An aspect of the cultural setting of a work***
  For example, a musical candidate researched the use of the piano and household music in Jane Austen's time, performed a typical piece on the piano, and discussed the role and use of music in *Pride and Prejudice*. Another candidate made a CD of the various types of music and pieces in *A Streetcar Named Desire* and played extracts, accompanied by a discussion of the New Orleans traditions and the popular music of the time, and the effect of the music in the play.

- ***A thematic focus***
  A candidate presented different attitudes towards marriage in *Pride and Prejudice*, illustrated with readings of passages.

- ***Characterization***
  A candidate analysed some different ways in which characters are presented and used in *Great Expectations*. Another wrote an imagined diary of *Hedda Gabler* during the action of the play and performed it as a powerful monologue.

- ***Techniques and style***
  A candidate compared the use of symbols in *The Scarlet Letter* and *The Glass Menagerie*.

- ***Interpretation of particular elements from different perspectives***
  A candidate took the roles of three different characters from *Pride and Prejudice* (Mr Collins, Elizabeth and Mrs Bennet) and presented their views of marriage 'in character', using their perspective and style.

The forms in which such topics might be presented

- *An orderly statement of facts*, for example: an introduction to a work, the setting of a work, an author.

- *A commentary*, for example on the use of an image, or on an extract from a work.

- *A comparison* of two passages, or two characters, or two works.

- *An imitation* of a poem or prose style, followed by an examination of the original and an analysis of your imitation.

- *An invented monologue* by a character during or after the action of a work.

- *Role play*: an author explaining or defending his/her work; or a character explaining or defending his/her position.

Think which of the above would be most interesting for you to do.

Some examples of memorable student presentations

- A student who composed and sang her own music wrote and performed a lyric that represented in sequence the feelings of the main characters in Tennessee Williams' *The Glass Menagerie*. She then explained, with close reference to the text, why she had given the characters the particular words they sang.

- A student compared Ted Hughes'and Sylvia Plath's poems on Wuthering Heights, both written after a visit there.

- A student looked at a poem in translation and in the original language, and considered what was gained or lost in translation.

- A student took Achebe's attack on the racism of Conrad's *Heart of Darkness*, and defended Conrad against the charge.

- A student compared how two writers treat heroism.

- A student compared two poems on the same theme: Donne's "Death Be Not Proud" and Emily Dickinson's "Because I could Not Stop for Death". The student recited both poems, partially acting them, then gave a presentation on the respective treatments of the theme.

- A student gave a commentary on the most challenging chapter (14) in Primo Levi's *If This Is A Man,* placing it in the context of the whole work.

- A student created a map of walks in *Pride and Prejudice*, showing how each was strategic to the novel.

- A student wrote a monologue based on a section of Kafka's *The Trial*. He taped it, with different kinds of music accompanying different moods during the piece, and played it while he mimed the situation. He later answered questions about his character and actions.

- A student took the persona of a minor character in Primo Levi's *If this Is A Man,* who has been condemned to the gas chambers, and created a dramatic monologue, with a perceptive examination of what one would feel in those circumstances.

- Two poems on paintings were compared and discussed.

Once you have decided what you would like to do, discuss this briefly with your teacher to check that it is appropriate. Look at the descriptors (assessment criteria) carefully and ensure that what you have planned will allow you to demonstrate those qualities.

Remember that ten minutes of speaking demands a lot of preparation if it is to be sharp and persuasive. But DO NOT write it out as if an essay, or you will be trying to remember what you wrote and that is not an oral.

Instead, assemble your material, find a good order for it and way of presenting it, and make headings only. You will need to feel comfortable about and in control of your material if you are to maintain eye contact and compel your audience with your ideas. The key to this is planning and practice. Avoid being too technological, though simple visual aids and props can be helpful. This can be an enjoyable experience and others can learn a lot from it too.

1. Introduction

What are they?

World Literature Assignments One and Two (One only at Standard Level) are:

- assignments of 1,000 -1,500 words each
- based on your World Literature texts (details on this later)
- on topics chosen by you
- written in your own time
- supervised by your teacher but submitted to an external examiner at the end of February in the second year of the programme
- 20% of your final A1 grade
- designed to introduce you to cultures and literary traditions different from your own

The two assignments are different in kind. Descriptions of both are given below.

Since they are written in your time, and may be revised until you are satisfied, this is an area of the A1 programme over which you have some control, and it is worth going about the task carefully. It can make a difference to your final grade.

On the other hand, the essays are not PhD theses, and it is unnecessary to agonize unduly about the task. The assignments are similar to others that you have probably been producing throughout the two years. But they should be fulfilling for you, something you enjoy working on. Make the most of the wide choices available to you.

It is helpful if your teacher can give you photocopies of the regulations for the World Literature Assignments published in the Language A1 Subject Guide. This chapter gives you the essence of those regulations. In addition, a very useful document, "Language A1 World Literature", has been prepared by the IB as teacher support material. This provides, with examiner comments, many excellent samples of World Literature Assignments. Your teacher should have this and may share the contents with you.

When do you write them?

This varies from school to school and may depend on when the texts are taught. Some schools ask for World Literature Assignment One in the first year or over the summer of the first year. Others set a deadline in the first few months of the second year. The reason some teachers ask for the assignment in the first year is to avoid crowding the second year with tasks. On the other hand, your skills may not be as well developed in the first year and the assignment may not represent the quality you are capable of later, so you should revise it. World Literature Two is usually produced by December or January of the second year.

What is the teacher's role?

Your teacher is expected to help you find an appropriate topic (but not to assign you one) and ensure that you are proceeding in the right way to meet the requirements and the assessment criteria. S/he is supposed to read the first draft and may comment on it, orally, or by notes on a separate sheet. S/he must countersign the cover sheet of the final copy, confirming that it is your own work, and does not contain plagiarism.

The importance of more than one draft

It is unusual for candidates to produce a good assignment with the first draft, though it depends on the way you have prepared and your experience in writing such assignments.

Expect to write at least two or three drafts if you want to achieve your desired grade. As your teacher is only required to read the first draft, and may expect you to work independently from then on without further prodding or encouragement, it is up to you to take an interest in your work and revise it yourself. Use the assessment criteria and the checklist provided below to estimate your standards and the areas to improve.

If you have been asked to produce your first assignment in the first year, you should revise it later when your skills are more developed. Even if the teacher has your first draft in his or her filing cabinet, there is nothing to stop you working to perfect your assignment(s) on your own, and turning them in before the deadline. In fact you should do this.

What are examiners looking for in these assignments? What are the assessment criteria?

To understand this, the best thing is to ask your teacher for copies of the assessment criteria that examiners use when they are marking your work. These will also help you to evaluate your own work before submitting it. There are four criteria for each assignment, each worth a maximum of five points, as summarised below. The same criteria are used for both World Literature Assignments One and Two.

World Literature Assessment Criteria:

A: An appropriate, specific and clearly defined topic
   Independent ideas, well developed in relation to the topic, and showing personal response

B: Good knowledge of the works studied
   Detailed knowledge of and good insight into the aspect of the texts chosen
   Meaningful linking of works, and appreciation of similarities and differences
   Appreciation of the cultural setting, where appropriate

C: Effective, clear and logical structure
   Precise and pertinent references
   Within the word limit
   Statement of intent (as for WL 2 creative option) is clear, detailed and relevant

D: Clear written expression
   Conventions of written work (paragraphing, spelling, grammar) carefully observed
   Appropriate register (vocabulary, tone, sentence structure)

2. World Literature Assignment One: The Comparative Essay

What is it and what is it based on?

This is the same for Higher and Standard levels. It is a *comparative* essay based usually on *two* of your three Part One World Literature works. Make sure you know which these are. (Many students don't, at this point.) A typical school choice for Part One might be:

Example 1
A Doll's House by Ibsen
Antigone by Sophocles
The Cherry Orchard by Chekhov.

Example 2
House of the Spirits by Allende,
Anna Karenina by Tolstoy,
Chronicle of a Death Foretold by Marquez

A comparative essay can be a challenge because it may be the first time you have attempted such an assignment. If you see the task as a process involving several stages, as described below, it should be less daunting. The value of a comparative essay is that you see each text more clearly, in a more interesting perspective, when you relate it to the other. No text will be exactly like another in terms of a chosen aspect. Differences as well as similarities will be illuminating.

Common difficulties in World Literature Assignment One:

As you read the following, mark the areas that you think could be a problem for you:

- Selecting a specific, concrete topic
- Writing a clear introduction indicating the thesis or direction of the essay
- Developing a clear argument through the subsequent paragraphs
- Providing detailed supporting evidence for ideas
- Indicating an awareness of the culture and period
- Contrasting as well as comparing texts
- Demonstrating awareness of the literary (and dramatic) aspects of the texts
- Writing a sufficient amount
- Analysing or interpreting as opposed to merely describing

It is comforting to know that many of these problem areas can be avoided by some fairly simple strategies. Observing the following guidelines and suggestions should help you improve your standard in many of the areas.

How to find a good topic for Assignment One in Four Stages

Examiners are looking for something fresh, personal, persuasive. How do you accomplish this? Many students find it hard to come up with a good topic that genuinely links two works. It need not be too difficult, if you follow these stages.

Step One: Re-read your works

This is crucial! You are much more likely to come up with an interesting topic if you know your works well. Re-reading the works is one of the most important steps to success in this task. The topic should emerge from your close reading of the text; it shouldn't be an idea that you impose on the text.

A second reading of a work is always a very different experience from the first reading, which tends to be piecemeal, in stages, often spread over several weeks. Plays, short novels or poetry you should try to re-read in one or two sittings. The reading will bring to mind ideas discussed in class that helped you understand the work better, but should also bring fresh ideas, things you hadn't noticed before. (It may be helpful, before you re-read, to review sections of Chapter Two: How to Study Texts.) Look for:

- Patterns
- Points of emphasis
- The logic of development
- Details
- Particularly vivid passages

If your works are very long (*Anna Karenina*, for example), it may be impossible to re-read them entirely though it is still desirable. Be prepared for this by reading the assigned chapters or sections twice during the in-class study:

- The first time look for the overall effect and narrative
- The second time make more detailed notes

- Add to your notes when you discuss it in class (and when you revise, if you have time for this)
- Make a note of passages you particularly like or find interesting. These notes may become the basis for a topic later, as they did for the student who compared the deaths of Madame Bovary and Santiago Nasar in Marquez's *Chronicle of a Death Foretold*.

Re-reading the texts as described above is essential to:

- Finding a good topic (Criterion A)

- Strengthening your knowledge and understanding of works and your insights (Criterion B)

- Expressing and structuring your ideas. The better your grasp of the text, the more confident your expression and structure will be (Criterion C)

- Writing clearly. Really having something to say improves the quality of your writing (Criterion D)

Know your genre and its characteristic features

In re-reading your works, be aware of the characteristics of the genres of your text, of their literary features (in the case of drama, dramatic features also) and how these work. Many students study drama for Part One, yet read the texts as if they were novels rather than texts written to be brought alive on stage. Chapter Two: How to Study Texts, and sections of Chapter Three: The Examination Essay, will help you with this, as will the Glossary. These features can provide good topics.

Step Two: Find a starting point; connect with your interests or responses

The lucky link

You may be lucky or observant and find a good link quickly, like the candidate who spotted that there was a medical operation in both *Chronicle of a Death Foretold* and in *Madame Bovary*, and that there were interesting similarities between these; or like another candidate in the same class who saw that sleep was frequently referred to in both novels, and explored this topic. (Both these are illustrated below).

The 'four-moment' test

If such links are not obvious in your case, try thinking about which text you have enjoyed most, and quickly, spontaneously write down at least four moment or aspects that stand out in your memory about it. Something about a character, or about the way the work is written, or a particular episode or image? Reflect on why these moments or features stand out, and write down your comments. Choose the ones that appeal to you most and see if they are can be linked with one of your other Part One texts? For example, one candidate was interested in the 'cunning' of Ivan Denisovitch, and how this drew the reader's sympathy. She then found that Nora in *A Doll House* could also be described as cunning, and began to look at similarities of the authors' purposes in creating them like that, and the effects achieved.

Your personal interests

Another way to find a topic is through your own interests, like the student-photographer who was fascinated by the use of doors and windows in *Hedda Gabler* and *Three Sisters*. Another artistic candidate starting thinking about what she responded to visually in her plays, and found that two of her plays had patterns of earth and sky imagery, but with very different effects (illustrated below). A third, student-actor noticed how much the two main female characters in *The Cherry Orchard* and *Hedda Gabler* laughed in their plays, but for different reasons and with different effects.

However well the topic works for one text, though, if it does not work for the second, you need to come up with another idea. A strained or unconvincing link will damage the assignment.

As you begin work on your topic, think of these questions:

- What is the *role* of your chosen aspect (eg, sleep) in these works?
- How does this differ or seem the same when comparing the texts?
- What effects do they create in the text?
- What was the authors' probable purpose in placing them there?

If your topic is clear, it will be easier to move on to the next stage of assembling the evidence and moving towards the thesis.

Will secondary sources help at this stage?

You are not given any credit for a bibliography of secondary sources for these assignments, unlike the Extended Essay. The majority of good and outstanding World Literature essays are written without benefit of such material, and are based purely on the texts. Many students do not know their texts in enough depth, so your priority should be reading these carefully, not reading about them.

As your argument and ideas are supposed to be based on your *personal* reading of your works, others' ideas may confuse or interfere with the coherence of your response. This is usually very obvious (and annoying) to an examiner. Internet sources are indeed readily available and a temptation to use, but you need to be aware of the meaning and consequences of plagiarism (losing your whole Diploma) and attribute any sources that you use in your bibliography. You *are* given credit, on the other hand, for your *independent* ideas and *personal* response.

However, there are some ways in which secondary sources may be of some benefit. In order to understand your works well, to write about them appropriately, you should be aware of the period and cultures the authors were working in. This includes the prevailing conditions, *mores* and attitudes of those times and places.

You should be aware (in the case of drama) of the theatrical conditions and characteristics, and as far as possible, the authors' intentions. Did Sophocles expect his audience to sympathise with *Antigone*? What did he believe about the Gods? How have different generations responded to these works? Works or articles that give you these kinds of insights can provide a valuable, even desirable perspective or sharper edge to your knowledge. Some sources that may help in these ways are provided in the bibliography in Chapter Two.

You should cite the edition of your texts for the benefit of the examiner, as translations may vary.

Step Three: Identify a suitable topic for World Literature One

A good topic is:

- Specific and concrete (not vague and abstract)
- One that preferably has a literary focus or shows awareness of literary aspects (the particular characteristics of novels, plays and poetry)
- One that recognises how the author has deliberately constructed the text, with reasons for his/her choices, rather than treating the text as 'life' (eg. "How the elderly are used in *House of the Spirits* and *Anna Karenina*")
- One that is yours, not your teacher's, or identical with anyone else's in your class

Look at the following list

Decide which topics are appropriate. If you think any of them is unsuitable, jot down your reasons.

---

a. "How Nora and Medea throw off male oppression in Ibsen's *A Doll's House* and Euripides' *Medea*"

b. "Earth and sky imagery in Sophocles' *Antigone* and Chekhov's *Three Sisters*"

---

c. "The history of Chile in Allende's *The House of the Spirits* and Dorfman's *Death and the Maiden*"

d. "The impact of narrators of offstage action in Sophocles' *Antigone* and Ibsen's *Hedda Gabler*"

e. "Blindness and sight in Durrenmatt's *The Visit* and Sophocles' *Oedipus Rex*"

f. "Yesterday and still today"

g. "Love and death in Tolstoy's *Anna Karenina* and Flaubert's *Madame Bovary*"

h. "A comparison of the treatment of the deaths of Emma in *Madame Bovary* and Santiago Nasar in *Chronicle of a Death Foretold*"

i. "Dramatic irony, suspense and foreshadowing in *Oedipus Rex* and *The Cherry Orchard*"

j. "The alienation of the central character from society in *Metamorphosis* and *Anna Karenina*"

k. "Are Nora and Medea justified in their actions and do we have sympathy for them?"

Comments on the above titles:

a. Is a popular but potentially dangerous kind of topic, because it could easily, using a modern feminist perspective, ignore cultural, time and literary differences, treat characters as real, and depend more on opinion than critical awareness. It also suggests a reductive, even erroneous view of Medea's role.

b. Is specific and literary and so is appropriate

c. Is historical rather than literary in focus

d. Focuses on a specific dramatic feature, and so is appropriate

e. Treats the symbolism of the characterisation and theme, and is specific, literary and appropriate

f. Is vague and does not clearly indicate a topic

g. Is far too broad. "The treatment of married love" would be more appropriate

h. Is specific and appropriate

i. Has too many subjects. If the title were adapted to something like "How suspense is created by dramatic irony and foreshadowing", the different elements might be successfully combined

j. Is an overworked topic that tends to be too broad, dull and abstract. It is best to try to avoid topics that have 'alienation' and 'society' in them

k. There is nothing 'wrong' with a topic that is presented as a question (though avoid multiple questions). It may help you to keep focused when you are exploring and structuring your ideas, as with the Extended Essay. It also helps you test your idea and genuinely address evidence that might contradict it. But there is no obligation to present the final title in this way. You can always turn your question back into a statement at this stage. Thus "What is the role and effect of weapons in *Chronicle of a Death Foretold* and *Hedda Gabler*..." becomes "The role and effect of weapons in...".

Step Four: Assemble the evidence

Before you can develop ideas on your topic, you need to collect the 'evidence', the references or quotations relating to your topic. Then look for patterns and develop some ideas from these. This should follow your re-reading (Step One). Students have found the careful assembling of evidence an invaluable way to shape their assignments. It is also the stage at which you can see if your proposed topic is going to work and to hold your interest.

You cannot analyse (seeing how parts relate to the whole) until you see the whole picture. An analytical approach is what distinguishes the good performance from the mediocre. Students often complain that their teachers tell them to be 'more analytical', to stop 'telling the story'. How is this to be done? Think of it as a three-stage process:

- Read and understand the text (see Step One above)
- Select a topic, and collect and comment on illustrations or quotations that seem significant and interesting in relation to this topic (see grid, p.89-90)
- Find a way to organize these comments and ideas into a meaningful statement or argument (see Angela's thesis below)

The 'Grid' is one way to do it, which many students have found helpful, though you may find another method that works better for you.

Making a grid of evidence

- Take a double spread of two A4 sides, and make 3 columns on each page (6 in total)
- In the first column ('Quotes') list quotations on your topic with page references from text one
- In the second column ('Comments'), jot down comments on each reference
- When you have done that, read through the quotations and comments. Is a pattern emerging? Do they connect in groups?
- Try to come up with at least three ideas or an analysis that you write in the third column ('Analysis')
- In the fourth, fifth and sixth columns do the same for the second text
- Now look across the 'Analysis' columns especially, for overall patterns of similarities and differences between the text
- Now you can start to put together a thesis and introductory paragraph

The advantages of the grid:

The example below shows how this may be done. There are several advantages to this method:

- The concrete nature of the quotations roots your ideas closely in the text and helps you avoid the temptation to vagueness and abstraction.

- It also helps you see all your evidence at one glance, so that patterns are more striking. You will usually find you have more references than you need for purposes of quoting, but seeing them connected will provide a better grasp of the topic.

- It helps you progress from description (ie. "This is what happens") to comment ("These are my responses and ideas") and finally to analysis ("This is how the topic relates to the broader picture and how the two texts compare"). Many students find the leap to 'analysis' difficult but this process can assist that development.

- It enables you to see that there is sufficient material for you to write about in both texts, and that the link is workable. This helps solve the problem of having enough to write about. Many candidates' work is too short.

How Angela did it:

Here is an example across the double page spread used by a student working with the topic of food and meals in *Metamorphosis* and *Anna Karenina*.

Angela's Grid

Anna Karenina

Quotes	Comments	Analysis
1. "The worst moment had been when, returning home from the theatre, merry and satisfied, with an enormous pear in his hand for his wife, at last he found her…with the unlucky note." (p. 2)	The pear is a reflection of his character (thinking of his wife, though dining and enjoying life separately from her) and adds to the foolishness of the figure he cuts here. Brilliant mix of comic-tragic.	-Characters lead divided lives. Food not a uniting element except with peasants and children. Reflects decline of societal values
2. (The day after that) "Having finished his second cup of coffee and a buttered roll..he smiled joyfully". (Meanwhile his household is in disarray, the cook gone, one child sick with sour broth, the others given "hardly any dinner.") (p. 7)	Oblonsky's 'civilized' pleasure in food, regardless of the situation. Epicurean. Division and contrast between one part of the household (his) and the rest.	- Simplicity and wholesomeness valued over sophistication. Food with peasants sacramental.
3. (Extended description of Levin and Oblonsky at a restaurant dinner) "'Not bad', said Oblonsky, pulling the quivering oysters out of the pearly shells with a silver fork, and swallowing one after another… Levin could eat oysters, though he preferred bread and cheese." (p. 32-5)	The scene works on many levels. A comment on the tension between French influence and Russian culture, and Russian rural values (hedonistic versus more spiritual values associated with the idea of the nobility of rural work). The dinner and surroundings seen ambivalently. Levin uncomfortable.	- Food used expressively to express social and spiritual values as well as character
4. (Levin mowing with his peasants. Children bring their fathers kvas and bread for dinner). "'The men began to preparing for their dinner. Some had a wash. The young lads bathed in the river. Others unfastened their bags of bread and unstopped their jugs of kvas. The old man broke some rye bread into a bowl, poured over it some water... then turning to the East, said grace. 'Come master, have some of my dinner", said he'". (p. 250)	A key passage, and good contrast with the above (no 3). Eating not solitary and divided. Women have prepared it, children bring it. Important ritual of the working day. Food a blessing (grace) and to be shared. No hierarchy or division between man and master. Daily bread cherished. Meal sacramental. Seems dear to Tolstoy's heart. No sense of the critical. Lovingly recounted.	
5. (Levin's visit to the old man's farm) "On departure, he found the whole peasant family at dinner. The women served standing. The vigorous young son with his mouth full of buckwheat porridge was saying something funny and everybody laughed heartily. There was an impression of welfare that this household produced on Levin; that impression was anyhow so strong that he never lost it. And all the way to Sviyazhsky's he every now and then recalled that household, as if the impression it left on him demanded special attention." (p. 321)	Another key passage, related to (4) but focusing on the welfare and unity of the family. The only family meal in the book. Exudes healthy living and togetherness. Interesting that the image speaks for itself. No thought process of Levin's shown, but no doubt of the value this has for him.	
6. (Grisha, Dolly's son, is denied pudding for a trivial offence. His sister on pretext of taking food for her doll, takes him some pudding in the nursery.) "He ate the pudding, muttering between sobs, 'eat some yourself..let us both eat together.'" (p. 260)	Children in this novel reflect parents' shortcomings or pretensions, inadequacies of upper-class parenting. Anna's son similarly upbraided for offence of eating peaches secretly. Levin criticises Dolly's parenting, and she is concerned about them. Children eat separately. Parents preoccupied with their affairs. Sister's and brother's natural impulse to share and express love and kinship.	

Angela's Grid

Metamorphosis

Quotes	Comments	Analysis
1. "His immediate intention was to get up quickly and above all to eat all his breakfast" (p.2)	Reference to the reassuring routine of family meals. Incongruous as he is now an insect. Irony and kind of humour	Food should be both nourishing and unifying element in family. Meals together
2. "The breakfast dishes were set out on the table lavishly... for Gregor's father lingered over it for hours..." (p.21)	A familiar old world. Contrast of father's leisure, G's world of work. Change to come for father too. Gregor separated, behind door.	Food/meals suggestive of orderliness and normality, also caring, love
3. "Gregor could not resist snapping his jaws together at the sight of the creaming coffee." (p.24)	Bridge between old G and new insect/ Greg. Incongruity, grotesque but also comical.	G's 'meals' show division/isolation; dislocation; stress new state
4. "To find out what he liked, she (Greta) brought him a whole section of food, all set out on an old newspaper...old, half decayed vegetables... he sucked greedily on the cheese." (p.29)	Crucial passage – part of fuller transition to insect status. Compare with 3.	Careful *structure of references* shows change, neglect, decline Ref. To food, part of meaning of whole
5. "Gregor came to a stop in alarm... for his father was determined to bombard him...was now shying apple after apple... another landed right on his back and sank in. G wanted to drag himself forward, as if this startling, incredible pain could be left behind him." (p.44)	Fruit, apples, normally positive, healthful. Part of orderly household, in a 'dish on the sideboard'. Here displaced, wrongful use as weapon of ultimate destruction. Father – killer.	Effects: concreteness, physicality of the food references, links story with our familiar world, provides strange contrast with horror
6. "At other times, he was only filled with rage at the way (his family) were neglecting him. He would make plans for getting into the larder to take food that was after all, his due." (p.48)	Increasing neglect, but G's human feelings remain. Food – measure of love or lack of it.	Same setting throughout emphasises change in relation to food Patterns emerging? -Contrast between unity (before) and division (now) -Anguished isolation - power of the 3rd person limited -The physicality of home setting and food -food references tell us something about the characters.
7. "Gregor was now hardly eating anything" (p.50)	Food – measure of his will to live or not	
8. (lodgers and their food) "'I'm hungry enough', said G sadly to himself, 'but not for that kind of food. How these lodgers are stuffing themselves, and here I am dying of starvation". (p.51)	Changes. Lodgers have displaced family in dining room. Gregor further distanced. Effect of unusual direct speech. His human voice. Food as emotional nourishment.	

Angela's thoughts on this process:

To be honest, I had no idea how I was going to find a good link between these two very different novels. I started by reading Metamorphosis. On this re-reading I noticed the food much more than the first time. We hadn't discussed food in class, but it really stood out. When I had collected as many quotes as possible I read them in sequence, and the way each related to the next was very striking. My comments and responses came very quickly. The passage about the father throwing apples and the apple that rotted in the back were the scenes that I remembered most from my first reading and I wanted to be able to include them, because I wanted the chance to explore why I reacted so strongly to them.

I was a bit afraid of tackling Anna Karenina again, because of length, and I wasn't sure there were many references to food, but when I started I found some really interesting scenes that I knew I wanted to focus on. My favourite was Oblonsky's pear. I had to find a way to work this into the essay. However, the significance of these scenes was so very different from the other text that it took me a while to find a way to relate them. This was the hardest bit of this exercise. I finally found a link that I thought worked. The key word for me, looking at all the evidence, was isolation. Once I'd got this starting point, I could work out the similarities and differences and shape this into a thesis statement. (Quoted below)

Moving towards a thesis or argument

Some students have had practice in this for years; others have never done it before and find it one of the most challenging aspects of this assignment. However, if you can master the skill now, you will find it invaluable for many future tasks. Knowing the texts well, and assembling the evidence systematically, as Angela has done here, is a necessary foundation.

Once you have your evidence, look first at the role your topic plays in each text then look for similarities and contrasts. Let's see what Angela came up with:

Angela's thesis: *The significance of meals in Kafka's <u>Metamophosis</u> and Tolstoy's <u>Anna Karenina</u>*

Meals are not only necessary nourishment, but also provide occasions to experience the pleasure and strength of a group's unity. As something shared, as something to be grateful for, they can even have a sacramental significance. The pattern of references to meals in these texts do hint at this perspective, through glimpses of a happier past in <u>Metamorphosis</u> to rare moments showing the wholesomeness of peasant life in <u>Anna Karenina</u>. The emphasis in scenes describing meals and food in both novels, however, falls on the isolation and displacement of family members, even of food itself. This has a different significance in each novel. In <u>Metamorphosis</u> food references stress Gregor's anguished isolation from his family, his former source of comfort, security and love; in <u>Anna Karenina</u> they tend to show the disintegration or corruption of social, spiritual and family values.

---

3. How to Write the Assignment: Four areas for focus

(1) The introductory paragraph: thesis statement, argument or statement of aims
(2) How to compare: the structure of the whole essay
(3) The well-developed paragraph; referring to the text
(4) The conclusion

Much of the following is relevant to World Literature Assignment Two (especially the essay on a single topic and the comparative option).

(1) The introductory paragraph and thesis

The previous section on assembling and analysing evidence has shown how you move towards the thesis or argument, which should form the core of your introductory paragraph. The essential characteristic of the introduction is that it should lead on from the title to indicate clearly:

- the link between the texts
- the line of argument or exploration to be taken in the essay.

There is no one formula that is right in doing this. Some introductions provide a broad outline of the direction to be taken; others give a fuller and more concrete thesis that amounts to a conclusion. If you do this as in example (c) below, you need to be careful that there is still something new to say in the conclusion.

Compare the following examples and note your own responses to them before reading the comments given in the text.

(a) *Sleep: an exploration of the writers' use of this "simple human weakness" in Flaubert's <u>Madame Bovary</u> and Marquez's <u>Chronicle of a Death Foretold.</u>*

At the end of <u>Madame Bovary</u>, Homais, the pharmacist philosopher, and Bournisien, the town priest, fall asleep over the body of Emma Bovary, " coming together... in the same simple human weakness" (p.272). Both Flaubert and Marquez use this 'simple human weakness' to develop their characters, and reinforce the atmosphere of the provincial towns in which their stories are set. Perhaps most importantly, however, sleep in each novel is used to portray human imperfection.

90

We could describe this as 'the three-pronged thesis'. The candidate has identified three main ways in which the idea of sleep is used in each book, indicating a sound basis for comparison. The introduction is brief but effective, beginning with an interesting phrase ("simple human weakness") describing a specific moment in one of the texts, which was the starting point or trigger for this exploration. From the outset, we are specifically and concretely grounded in these texts. The structural framework for the development of the essay is clearly set: each of the three 'prongs' will be described and illustrated. We might say this essay treats a 'thematic' aspect, appropriately looking at its 'role' and 'significance' in the work.

(b) *Untergangsmusik: the death throes of power in Ibsen's <u>Hedda Gabler</u> and Chekhov's <u>The Cherry Orchard</u>.*

The music of downfall or "Untergangsmusik" is described as wild, ecstatic and despairing, like the medieval dance of death, whirling faster and faster in a circle, sure to end in demise. It is self-destructive, and has already gathered too much momentum: demise is inevitable. Both in Chekhov's <u>The Cherry Orchard</u> and Ibsen's <u>Hedda Gabler</u>, we hear the echoes of this music of downfall, as the power of the heroines is in its death throes. Each of these women makes a last despairing stand, which involves actual music, in an effort to manifest her power, but with this last manifestation she loses the causes of her power, and thus her power. They are, however, unable to do otherwise. If they do not manifest their power, they are lost, and if they do, they must fall. This manifestation of power itself is in the pattern of the music of doom, as it too is wild, brave, and leads to inevitable ruin.

This is a sophisticated approach that begins with seeing an analogy between a concept in German culture (*Untergangsmusik*) and the pattern of events in these plays, focusing on the characters of the female protagonists. The first two sentences define and amplify the idea of "untergangsmusik" to make the analogy clear. The introduction shows a firm and holistic grasp both of the two plays, and of the two women characters. The introduction goes further than example (a) as it gives a short analysis of the psychological state of the women, which will be developed in the essay. However, it does not go beyond the boundaries appropriate to an opening paragraph.

We might call this approach 'the single proposition'. It sets up a single idea that links the texts (the courage of the last hopeless stand of these women, analogous to the music of downfall), which will be demonstrated through close analysis of the texts. The focus will necessarily be on character analysis and comparison of those characters.

(c) *Earth and sky imagery in Sophocles' <u>Antigone</u> and Chekhov's <u>Three Sisters</u>*

Nature can have a profound effect upon a person's psyche: it can stir powerful emotions, or inspire significant thoughts and ideas. It has often been the basis of an artist's vision, and has played a prominent part in poetry and novels. It is not an aspect that springs to mind so quickly, perhaps, when thinking of plays, yet natural images can play a very important part in the meaning and characterisation of a play. In both <u>Three Sisters</u> and <u>Antigone</u> there is a pattern of references to earth and sky, but in each play these operate differently. In Chekhov such images reflect the many moods and emotions the characters feel; whereas in Sophocles they act as a connecting device between humans and Gods, reminding us of man's limitations and mortality, his inferiority to the Gods, anchoring our attention in the serious issues and debates at the heart of the play.

This is a 'literary' topic, an examiner's delight. The paragraph moves carefully from a broad approach to Nature images in the opening two sentences, to a focus on their relevance to those two plays in the third. Once the link of earth and sky images has been made, a *contrast* is indicated, a clear difference in the way images function, rather than a similarity. This is an important reminder that contrasts may be legitimately explored within a chosen aspect. You may feel that the last sentence provides too much analysis at this stage, and that it could end with "humans and Gods", leaving the rest to be used as paragraph topics.

> **(d) Under the Knife: a study of the authors' use of medical procedures to dissect characters and develop themes in Marquez's <u>Chronicle of a Death Foretold</u> and Flaubert's <u>Madame Bovary</u>.**
>
> *The autopsy of Santiago Nasar's body in <u>Chronicle of a Death Foretold</u> and the operation on Hippolyte's foot in <u>Madame Bovary</u> are medical procedures used to highlight the inabilities of Father Amador and Charles Bovary, and undermine their characters and authority within their societies. The unsuccessful operations are tied in with many recurrent themes of the novels and are crucial in the development of both plot and characterization.*

The candidate has given a 'creative' title ("Under the Knife"), and an informative subtitle to indicate the framework of the topic. This is worth mentioning because students often like to present a clever or witty title that does not clearly indicate the topic; a subtitle in such cases as here can do the work of a more conventional title. 'Cute' titles however should be avoided.

This opening demonstrates another complex or several-pronged thesis, as in example (a), but is interesting because the starting point is the similarity between two key scenes or episodes in the novels, which are then explored for their relation to the whole text. We may note that although several aspects of the topic are indicated, the candidate does not give provide conclusions, as do some of the previous examples.

If you compare this example (d) with the previous one (c), you will see that (d) states the direction of the topic in more general terms, leaving the candidate to become more specific in the body of the essay. Example (c) is much more explicit, outlining the argument which will then be demonstrated. Both approaches can be effective.

(2) The structure of the whole essay: how to compare the two texts

Students often ask how they should structure their comparison: dealing with the first text, then the second, or taking each point in turn and illustrating it in relation to both texts? Much depends upon the nature of the thesis or topic. A 'three-pronged' thesis may lend itself to the point-by-point comparison of texts (as illustrated below in the paragraph on the apple and pear in *Metamorphosis* and *Anna Karenina*). A comparison of key scenes as in "Under the Knife", example (d) above, is successfully treated by developing discussion on one scene and then the other, but keeping the comparison in mind throughout.

If the lines of argument and points of comparison are clearly drawn in the introductory paragraph (as in the case in the essay on "Sleep" below), and the subsequent paragraphs follow those lines closely, the comparison can be kept to the fore, even if the focus is on one text and then the other in the first half. The texts can then be brought together, as the "Sleep" essay demonstrates, and the danger of producing two separate mini-essays is avoided.

Brief references using 'cohesive devices' or 'hooks' such as "Unlike in *Madame Bovary*..." or "Whereas in *Chronicle of a Death Foretold*..", help keep the comparison in mind when dealing with the other text.

There is no one ideal formula. The assignment that is persuasive and effective, whichever way it is structured, with the line of argument driving the writing, and quotations supporting it, will be the successful one.

Sample of Assignment One (Higher Level)

Read the following example carefully with these qualities in mind. As you read, or when you have finished, jot down some of the elements that you think are successful or persuasive, or what you think may be lacking.

> **Sleep – an exploration of the writer's use of this "simple human weakness" in <u>Madame Bovary</u> and <u>Chronicle of a Death Foretold</u>.**
>
> *At the end of <u>Madame Bovary</u>, Homais, the pharmacist philosopher, and Bournisien, the town priest, fall asleep over the body of Emma Bovary, "coming together... in the same simple human weakness" (p.*

272). Both Flaubert and Marquez use this "simple human weakness" to develop their characters, and reinforce the atmosphere of the provincial towns in which their stories are set. Perhaps, most importantly however, sleep in each novel is used to portray human imperfection.

Flaubert uses sleep to define the weakness in his character, Charles, in Madame Bovary. Even as a boy, sleep was one of his dominant characteristics. He did not possess any great intelligence and ' fell asleep', during his lessons, as did the curate his tutor 'snoring away, mouth wide open'. At boarding school, ' he slept well in the dormitory'. Later, as a country doctor, called in the night by his first patient, he cannot help but fall asleep as he rides to him. "He tried to bring to mind all the fractures that he knew … his mind clouding with fatigue, and sleep coming down upon him again, he soon entered a state of drowsiness" (p.9). This suggests that he lacked the ability to concentrate, causing him to sleep away his problems, dismissing them from his life. This may be to his advantage when Emma becomes involved with her various men. Although he does not realize it, he hides himself from the truth through his sleep, and therefore cannot see that his wife is having an affair, sparing himself depression. When he comes home to Emma, he "munched an apple, finished off the wine, then went up to bed, lay down on his back and began to snore" (p.32). Charles is contented with a day of routine and does not yearn to experience everything, as his wife does. He chooses sleep over experiences, making him a dull, but very natural character in this novel.

This lack of personality is demonstrated to Emma, and to the reader, by the amount he sleeps: she is always found "next to a slumbering Charles". (p.42) The author makes Emma's feelings of hatred towards Charles understandable, for he is too easily pleased and not awake enough to experience life. He does not live up to the romanticised ideals that she has read of in novels. Like any human, he has his imperfections, unlike the characters in her books, and so can never live up to her expectations. "Oh why, at least, didn't she have for a husband one of those ardent taciturn men who work at their books all night, and finally, at sixty, when the rheumatism comes on, wears a string of medals" (p.48) Through sleep, Flaubert emphasises the banality of Charles behaviour, an unfledged trait in novels of that time.

Flaubert is famed for his unadorned representation of average life. By describing Emma's town as sleepy, the author has doomed the characters to being so also. It is that which leaves Emma feeling trapped and bored. After searching with no avail for life, all that is left is to conclude that "the village was asleep" (p. 67) and had no thought of ever coming alive. "Would this misery last forever? Would she never issue from it?" (p. 67) Sleepiness, which makes everyone human, and is the town's drawback, is a part of reality that Emma has yet to accept.

Chronicle of a Death Foretold encounters sleep in a different way; however, it still portrays human weakness. The day of the murder, most characters are described as "a little sleepy" because of the marriage celebrations which had taken place throughout the night before, and because of getting up for the early arrival of the bishop. It is specifically mentioned that Santiago Nasar, who is to be murdered that morning, "had slept little and poorly" (p.2). This explains why many thought when they saw him that "he already had the face of a dead man" (p.112). The fact that he had not had a good night's sleep ensured that he would not have much energy on this crucial morning. After dreaming of timber trees "for an instant he was happy in his dream" (p.1), but "when he awoke he felt completely spattered with bird shit". Waking with such an impression sparks uneasiness, does not forecast a good day. Santiago not only slept poorly that evening, but most nights, because "he always slept the same way his father had slept, with the weapon hidden in the pillowcase" (p.3). As sleep is a time when one should feel a sense of security, Santiago evidently could never sleep with complete ease (a comment on that culture of weapons but also ironically contrasting his vulnerability later that morning). "He always got up with the face of a bad night" (p.7). Sleepiness was what caused his confusion when returning home from the bishop's visit with the Vicario twins after him. "All the many people he ran into… later remembered him as being a little sleepy" that morning, his last alive.

Sleep is repeatedly used whenever the Vicario twins are referred to in the novel. It was apparent to all the townspeople that "the men who were going to kill him had slept on the benches" in the square (p.13). They had not slept for three nights while celebrating their sister's marriage, and now, faced with the perilous task of killing Santiago to save their sister's honour, they fell asleep at dawn. This eliminated the urgency of committing the crime. It seems as though, like Charles in Madame Bovary, they are attempting to sleep away their problems, which would provide them with an excuse not to kill him. This "simple human weakness" could have foiled their plans, but "instinct awoke them completely when Santiago Nasar came out of his house".

The townspeople too were drowsy on the morning of the murder, which would affect their accounts of the events of that day. "It's just that I haven't had a minute's sleep (p.109) was typical of the excuses. People's judgement was slowed, and the twins left "without anyone noticing, sheltered by public exhaustion" (p.83). As in Madame Bovary, sleep is a "simple human weakness", and "public exhaustion" could have constituted that which killed Santiago: had people been more awake, they would have been *more aware of the events about to unfold. This may be compared with the fact that Charles' sleeping in Madame Bovary is one of the elements leading to Emma's death.*

In both novels, once the central character is dead, there is an inability to sleep in the characters responsible. In Madame Bovary we see that "Charles, lying awake, was still thinking of her" (p. 278), just as Justin, the one who gave her the arsenic, "was not sleeping" (p. 279). In Chronicle of a Death Foretold the narrator, having suffered the horror of his friend's death, which he had slept through, "didn't have the courage to sleep at the end of that oppressive time" (p. 77), and the twins "fell into an insomniac drowsiness". Sleep, the "simple human weakness" is no longer so simple because their guilty conscience is keeping them awake, despite their convictions about the absolute principle of saving honour. In fact, they fear sleep, "because as soon as they began to fall asleep they would commit the crime all over again". Pablo Vicario "suffered the frightful certainty that he wouldn't sleep ever again for the rest of his life" and told the narrator he was awake for eleven months. Even many years later he said "It was like being awake twice over" (p. 79). In contrast to this, ironically the men Emma Bovary cared most about, who are as guilty as Charles and Justin though they do not feel it, do not care, and hence can sleep. "Rudolphe...was sleeping peacefully in his chateau; and Leon, far away, was asleep" (p. 278).

Sleep, indeed a human weakness, is distinctively rendered in both novels. This flaw in human nature is used by Flaubert to imprint the humanness and ordinariness of his character Charles, and by Marquez to mould the plot and give the community a collective reason for its failure to act. In both novels sleep comes to represent imperfection in human nature. (1485 words)

Comments on the sample

Having noted some responses to the above essay, as suggested on the previous page, now look back at the introductory section to this chapter, "What the Examiners are looking for" (p.83), and decide whether the candidate, in your opinion, has met these criteria.

In this assignment, having clearly defined the link between the novels in the introduction (a several-pronged statement or thesis), the candidate develops and supports this thesis in relation to one text, then the other. In the last two main paragraphs, continuing to develop her thesis, she then compares and contrasts the two novels within the same paragraphs. Her strength is her ability to support her idea persuasively through precise, detailed and constant reference to the text, with smooth transitions between statements and quotes. She has obviously assembled, scrutinised and sorted her materials clearly, and adhered to her argument throughout. She has also, within the framework of this very specific topic, skilfully managed to show a broader understanding of both works.

It might be objected that there is more quotation than discussion and development of ideas, but as one Examiner has said, quotation can be a powerful part of argument. The conclusion might have been longer, relating the topic to the wider aims of the novelists. However, the candidate has an interesting idea, and has developed it firmly and fully. For the average candidate, this is not that easy to do, and she has done it very competently.

(3) The well-developed paragraph (including how to use quotes)

The structuring and development of paragraphs is often an area of weakness in these assignments, yet they constitute the body of the essay, so it is worth looking carefully at how they should work, at what they can achieve. Good paragraphing is the key to successful essay writing.

What is a paragraph exactly?

It is a unit of thought in which you make and support a statement or idea. It should:

- relate clearly to the introduction, supporting and developing the main statement(s) made there
- lead out of the previous paragraph, and into the next in a clear and logical way
- have *one* main idea or focus, illustrated and developed through close reference to the text
- look both backwards (to the argument), and forwards, opening up the texts to reveal individual insights into them

94

If you have already drafted your World Literature Assignment, check to see if your paragraphs do these things.

Though paragraphs anchor the essay to the argument, there should be no rigid formula. The paragraph is also the vehicle for exploring the text, for developing ideas and indicating personal response (qualities which are all too rare and yet need not be). So there is some flexibility about how they are constructed. Quite often the need to elaborate on a main point, or discuss one aspect, means that several paragraphs are devoted in sequence to the same point. Thus the candidate in sample (d) "Under the Knife" quoted above carries his analysis and discussion of Santiago Nasar's autopsy through four paragraphs (not illustrated here).

The way the texts are referred to, through quotation or interpretive summary, and the way that texts are compared within the paragraph, or in subsequent paragraphs, varies quite a bit. If you look back at the penultimate paragraph in the "Sleep" essay, you see that a main point is made about guilt, and this is then supported by brief quotations from each text in turn. In the following paragraphs, a more complex idea is suggested, which requires closer analysis of the passages under consideration.

Example A: Paragraph development in Angela's Assignment One Essay: *Meals and food in Metamorphosis and Anna Karenina*.

At key points in their novels, Tolstoy and Kafka both introduce single items of food that stand out strikingly for their displaced context or function: in *Anna Karenina* a pear, in *Metamorphosis* an apple. Whereas fruit is usually cheerfully comforting in its healthfulness, and even luxurious, in these cases the items, coming between two members of the family, take on quite other associations. The narrative standpoint, and the tactile nature of the references, also contribute to the powerful effect of these moments. In the opening chapter of *Anna Karenina* we are introduced to Oblonsky who, caught out in adultery three days earlier by a letter his wife had found, is sleeping in his study. He recalls the moment when his wife confronted him.

"The worst moment had been when, returning home from the theatre merry and satisfied, with an enormous pear in his hand for his wife, he did not find her in the drawing room, nor, to his great surprise, in the study, but at last saw her in the bedroom with the unlucky note which had betrayed him in her hand."

This produces an incongruous effect: the situation is serious, traumatic, even, from the wife Dolly's point of view, yet the huge, genitally-shaped pear Oblonsky is holding, renders him foolish and sympathetic at the same time. He seems caught eternally in that moment, unable to present the pear intended with typical goodheartedness for his wife, (a momento of the pleasant evening he had had away from her company), forced to hold it as she vehemently upbraids him. Tolstoy's narrative technique allows this moment its full impact. As we already know that his wife has found him out, there is a certain dramatic irony as we see him, in this recalled moment, wander unawares into this trap, holding the pear. Oblonsky himself makes no mention of it in his recollection. Instead, we experience a double vision: we feel with Oblonsky as we follow his thoughts remembering that evening; but we see the full-frontal image, as it were, of the contented, absurd, pear-holding Prince, through the eyes of the omniscient narrator.

We do not know what happens to the pear, but what happens to the fateful "small red" apple in *Metamorphosis* is unforgettable, rotting in Gregor's back over the course of weeks, 'an inflamed path around it, all covered with soft dust." The apple- throwing episode is both climax and turning point, the vehement explosion of his father's anger and frustration, and a cause of Gregor's eventual demise. The apples are moved swiftly from their position "in a dish on the sideboard", an image of domestic orderliness and nourishment, presumably typical of this bourgeois household, to become missiles in an act of unilateral aggression, "for his father was determined to bombard him". One apple "landed right on his back and sank in", a repulsively tactile image, yet necessary to our sense of Gregor's "startling, incredible pain" and to our sense of the "reality" of the story. As with Tolstoy's episode, our perception of this scene is complex, privileged to see each family member's isolation. Moving from the mother's and sister's points of view as they clear his room and suddenly catch sight of this indeterminate 'brown mass", to his father's (understandable but wrong) reading of the situation, to Gregor's hopeless attempts to convey his "good intentions" to his father, the omniscient reader has a helpless sense of tragedy, along with an almost comic sense of the absurd.

We may note a number of things about what this student does with her paragraphs. To make her link and comparison fully enough, she has to deal with each text in succession. She links the scenes with a 'topic sentence' or main point in the first paragraph, and provides a 'hook' between the paragraphs at the beginning of the second. Her main idea relates clearly back to her introductory thesis about isolation and displacement. The focus never moves away from the item of food referred to.

She quotes the Tolstoy episode in full, to give the flavour of the text. Most notably, she shows her own response to this, interpreting the scene through close engagement with it. You have the sense that she has entered into the reality of the scene with appreciation, has dwelt on it and explored it with pleasure, and has also been able to appreciate the techniques that produce such a memorable effect. This all shows the independence of thought that is too rare a quality in these assignments, yet is not in itself difficult to achieve if one reads closely enough. In the second paragraph a longer sequence of action from Kafka has to be compressed, and so brief quotes or references are woven into the narrative, along with interpretation of the scene and its effects.

The following example is from an assignment (comparing Dorfman's *Death and the Maiden* with *Chronicle of a Death Foretold*) on how women in traditional societies employ subtle tactics to exercise physical and emotional control over the otherwise dominant men. It has already been suggested that topics involving the rights and powers of women are often vague, depending more on opinion than cultural and literary awareness. This one shows both cultural and literary sensitivity, weaving interpretative summary (sentence 2), pertinent and persuasive quotes, and comment into an illustration of her topic.

Example B: Paragraph development in Assignment One Essay: *How Women Take Control in Death and the Maiden and Chronicle of a Death Foretold*

The character of Angela Vicario allows us an insight into the type of deceit used by women of her community to manipulate and fool the men. She divulges to her coven of women friends that she had lost her virginity prior to her wedding night. Instead of condemning her for this crime, together they concoct an elaborate plot, rescuing her from her anticipated disgrace, by instructing her to "give herself a drastic douche of alum water to fake virginity", and later to "stain the sheet so she could display it the following day" (p. 91). This example illustrates that although women felt compelled to play the game, they were more than able to master it to their advantage. This aspect of controlling the game is further explored as Angela accuses Santiago Nasar of being her lover, thus sealing his fate and condemning him to death. Angela knows that in a society where "affairs of honour are sacred" (p. 63), society will always demand retribution for any infringements upon such honour. In order to satisfy this need of society, Angela, having been given ultimate control, knowing she won't be questioned or doubted, provides such a culprit, although "no-one had believed it had really been Santiago Nasar" (p. 90). Marquez chooses to surround the situation with a dense ambiguity, to highlight this understated control. At the most crucial moment, when she is confronted and asked with whom she had been, she does not hesitate for long:

She looked for it in the shadows, she found it at first sight among the many, many easily confused names from this world and the other, she nailed it to the wall with her well-aimed dart, like a butterfly with no will whose sentence has already been written.

The use of the harsh image "nailed it to the wall with her well-aimed dart" emphasises the brutal effect of her accusations, while the comparison between Santiago and a butterfly implies his true fragility, innocence and vulnerability in the face of Angela. The way she is coldly able to condemn another to death suggests that she is in essence suppressing the most feminine qualities.

---

(4) Conclusions

Students often agonise too much about these in advance. Once the assignment has been satisfactorily developed, some final reflection should emerge from your exploration without too much struggle. This may involve some broader speculation that leads outwards, away from the body of the essay, as in example (a) below.

You should have moved on from the introduction. In other words, the conclusion is not a mere re-statement of the introduction, yet should refer clearly back to it.

Consider the following opening and concluding paragraphs on the topic:

Example A: *An individual is often able to survive through his own dreams, fantasies and aspirations": Is this statement true of <u>Hedda Gabler</u> and <u>Three Sisters</u>?*

Introduction

It has been stated that an individual often is able to survive through his own dreams, fantasies and aspirations, no matter how implausible their realization might seem. In the lives of the heroines of these two plays, their dreams and aspirations assume such importance that without the continued belief in and hope for them the characters cannot continue to live in a reality plagued with torment and hardship of various kinds, as they see and feel it.

****

Conclusion

In a sense, both the dreams of Hedda Gabler and the three sisters only serve their purpose when they are not fulfilled. These dreams are immortalized beyond all rational expectation. Perhaps Olga and her sisters come to realize this, so protecting themselves from the fate that caused the death of Hedda. Hedda's suicide, whether interpreted as courageous or cowardly, looks back, enshrining the dream she could never realise. The sisters, with their greater, Russian capacity for suffering, look forward, beyond the dream, bleakly sure of nothing but the necessity to endure.

We can see here how the concluding paragraph goes beyond the statement made in the introduction, speculating on the ambivalence of the plays' endings.

Example B: *A Sense of the Past: How reliable is the evidence of the senses in justifying revenge or conviction in <u>Death and the Maiden</u> by Dorfman and <u>The House of the Spirits</u> by Allende.*

Introduction

When a transition in government occurs, people are often trapped in the middle of turmoil; they are repressed and persecuted by the new regime. Isabel Allende and Ariel Dorfman, both Chilean authors, use the turmoil of the 1970's in Chile as a backdrop for their stories. Alba in <u>House of the Spirits</u>, and Paulina, the protagonist in <u>Death and the Maiden</u>, have similar experiences when detailed for "questioning". During their inquisition, physical senses – touch, smell, and hearing – are enhanced as a result of being blindfolded. In contrast, their sense of time is lost as they grasp for order in their solitude and isolation. Both authors show how the deprivation of one human sense serves to enhance another, and that the effect of sensory memory influences life. Each author leaves the reader facing the challenge: are memories of the senses enough to justify revenge and conviction?

****

Conclusion

The opportunity to live effectively in the present relates directly to a person's ability to let go of the past. Both Allende and Dorfman reveal the scars that the sensory memories of the past inflict on their characters. In contrast to Alba, Paulina's hatred drove her to devise an opportunity to kill her supposed perpetrator. Her perception of reality was skewed by her senses being continually reminded of the past. She believed that her senses were enough to convict Roberto and allow her to kill him. Innocence is inconsequential; she simply longs for vengeance. Allende assumes Alba was correct in her judgement of Colonel Garcia, but shows her ability to let go of the past and move on with her life. Dorfman leaves the reader to decide the psychological and moral dilemma: is evidence of a person's senses enough to convict someone of a crime? Or could the senses become distorted and deceive or mislead?

In Example B, whereas the introduction focused on the similarity of circumstances, the conclusion introduces a contrasting view of the women in the light of the essay's exploration, and a certain judgement or perspective on Paulina. The authors' challenge, presented in the introduction, is re-stated in the conclusion, but with a difference: the double question suggests stronger doubt about the reliability of the senses.

A checklist for your first draft of the World Literature Assignment One

As you sit down to write your first draft, you should be able to say 'yes' to the six questions in the first stage. The seven questions in stage two will serve both as reminders for what you need to remember as you write, and as a checklist on completion of the draft. If you cannot tick/check everything (and few people get it all right the first time) you now know what you need to work at.

First stage: sitting down to write

1. Have you carefully re-read the relevant Part One texts with a fresh eye and mind, making some new notes? Do you have a good grasp of the whole text as well as the parts you'll be using?

2. Have you looked through the assessment criteria to remind yourself what the examiner will be looking for?

3. Have you selected a clear, specific topic you can really explore with interest?

4. Have you assembled evidence from each text, as in "Angela's Grid", to ensure you have enough material and supporting evidence?

5. Have you looked back through examples of opening paragraphs to help you construct your thesis?

6. Are you aware of the times and cultures and different literary traditions in which your texts were written, and of the circumstances in which your authors produced their texts? Do you need to do some more background reading? A sense of these things will help you create an appropriate perspective.

Second stage: on completion of the draft

7. Have you really *compared* the works, or does your essay fall into two mini-essays, for example looking at bird imagery in this work, and then bird imagery in that, without exploring their similarities and differences? This is a *comparative* essay, remember. If you haven't done that, list your main ideas about each text and see where they are similar or dissimilar.

8. Are your main ideas and points carefully supported and illustrated with relevant and apt references to the text, or quotations? If not, find good ones and incorporate them. You need them for a convincing argument.

9. Is your essay more descriptive than analytical? Does it describe, for example, violence here and violence there, rather than analysing the part these moments of violence play in the whole. What effects do they create and how do they work in one text compared with the other?

10. Have you consulted secondary sources, including any from the internet, and used or quoted some of their ideas? If so, they need to be attributed. Remember, plagiarism can cost you your diploma.

11. Are you within the word limit? You will be penalized if you are more than 10% above or below the limit. Quotations must be included, though not footnotes or bibliography. Aim at 1,200 words at least.

12. Have you made a bibliography indicating the editions and translations of the texts you are using, as well as any other sources used?

4. World Literature Assignment Two

World Literature Assignment Two:

- is for Higher candidates only
- is assessed using the same criteria as for the first assignment
- has a variety of options
- is based on any of the five World Literature texts excluding those already used in Assignment One

When do you write it?

It is usually written in the second year, often between December and February. You should certainly have read all your World Literature works before you make your choice, to allow yourself the maximum advantage. It is possible that some written work or studying you have done earlier in the course may seem to you a good basis for an assignment (perhaps on a World Literature text that you read and enjoyed in the first year). This is fine, but you should re-read the text with a fresh mind for a good topic, and not rely on earlier work or ideas that may not be representative of your present capacities.

Three Options for World Literature Assignment Two

The options are described below, with comments and examples. They are also set out in the Subject Guide, and your teacher should give you copies of the relevant pages. The range of options gives you the possibility of writing in a form you enjoy and on a topic that suits your interests. It offers greater freedom of choice and individuality of approach than most other parts of the programme. Make the most of this opportunity. However, you should consider carefully which option will permit you to do justice to your skills. Although this assignment is often done extremely well, one of the main weaknesses is an unwise choice. More is written on this under the 'creative' option. Look carefully through the following sections and decide which would be best suited to your skills and experience.

1. A Comparative Study

This is based on *one* of your five World Literature texts (except those you have written on for World Literature One) and *any* other text in your A1 programme (ie: from Parts Two, Three and Four). This allows you to use a text you have really enjoyed, and opens up a large and unusual range of topics for comparison.

For example, one candidate wrote on the unlikely subject of "Manners in Solzenitsyn's *One Day in the Life of Ivan Denisovitch* and Jane Austen's *Pride and Prejudice*", another on "The effect of the structured day in *One Day* and Atwood's *The Handmaid's Tale*". A candidate whose favourite text was Hawthorne's *The Scarlet Letter* used this text to write on the impact of concealment in that novel and Ibsen's *A Doll's House*. Another candidate who enjoyed Shakespeare was able to write about bird imagery in Sophocles's *Antigone* and Shakespeare's *Macbeth* (illustrated below)

If you have struggled with the comparative essay for Assignment One, you probably won't want to tackle another such essay. But if you enjoy the challenge and opportunity this presents, you can create and explore unusual links between texts. Remember that, just as with Assignment One, the topic should be specific and literary.

The comparative essay is demonstrated in the section on World Literature One, so this type of essay, and the way to approach it, should be familiar to you. The following extract illustrates the combination of a World Literature text and a text 'from elsewhere in the programme', in this case Part Two.

Sample assignment of the Comparative Study (opening section only)

The Role of Bird Imagery in Shakespeare's <u>Macbeth</u> and Sophocles' <u>Antigone</u>

Birds have always had a profound effect on humans and have had similar meanings in different cultures. Both Sophocles and Shakespeare use bird images to define characters in extreme situations; birds suggest emotion in its purest form because they are instinctive. They also use references to birds to create or heighten mood at crucial moments, and to reveal truths through augury. The impact of the images in each play, however, is different. Shakespeare uses the images especially as part of the setting, to enhance the meaning and atmosphere; whereas Sophocles' images underline an intellectual debate.

Antigone and Lady Macbeth are compared to birds at moments when they are vulnerable, faced with the superior force of the masculine world. The soldier who catches Antigone when she finds her brother's body uncovered, suggests her wild grief when he describes the scene to Creon: she was "screaming like an angry bird, when it finds its nest empty and its little ones gone". The bird image underlines the instinctive untamed rage of the girl, but also her maternal instincts, wanting to protect her brother.

Similarly, Lady Macduff comparing herself with her husband who appears to have left his family without thought, describes herself in terms of "the poor wren (who) will fight, her young ones in her nest, against the owl". The tiny bird will fight a large bird of prey to protect her offspring, however hopeless. The metaphor clearly defines her courage and her maternal instinct, and intensifies the horror of the murder that is to come. Like his mother, her young son shows his innocent courage by asserting that he will fend for himself, as birds do, even if his father never comes back. Lady Macduff, with her adult understanding, sees him tenderly as a 'poor bird', vulnerable and exposed to danger and violence.

Birds in both plays are used to create mood, though very differently. In <u>Macbeth</u>, Act 1, scene VI, as Banquo enters Macbeth's castle,, he elaborates on the fact that the "temple-haunting martlet" has made a nest in the ramparts. He builds a moods of peacefulness and harmony, saying that where the bird builds, "heaven's breath smells wooingly", and "the air is delicate". But Shakespeare is creating dramatic irony: Banquo thinks that all is peaceful, while as the spectators know, the Macbeths are plotting Duncan's murder. Contrastingly, birds associated with darkness such as crows, ravens, the falcon, and owls are also used in connection with the murder, suggesting evil and horror. Lady Macbeth says that "the raven himself is hoarse" when Duncan is approaching, warning of impending death with his constant cry.

In <u>Antigone</u>, Creon's first reference to birds is that the corpse of Polynices is "to be left unburied, left to be eaten by dogs and vultures, a horror for all to see". This creates a feeling of horror at Creon's vindictiveness, and sympathy for Antigone whose brother's body is to be thus treated. Later, the prophet Teiresias's account of "birds in vicious combat" creates an atmosphere of outrage, indicating strongly that the behaviour of the birds, the messengers of the Gods, reflect the horror of Creon's deed in leaving Polynices' body unburied. "How should the birds give any other than ill-omened voices, gorged with the dregs of blood that man has shed?" In both cases, the natural universe cries out at what is done by man, or echoes the horror of it.

Comment on the sample

The candidate has found a way to incorporate a favourite text: *Macbeth*, into the World Literature assignments. She has chosen an unusual and valid topic linking the two plays and has found strong aspects of comparision, made persuasive through vivid quotations.

2. An Imaginative or Creative Assignment

This is based on one World Literature text or on a combination of one such text and a text from any part of the A1 programme. The Language A1 Subject Guide, which your teacher has, includes a list of suggestions as to the form this assignment might take. For example:

- a meeting between two characters from different works
- an extra chapter or scene in the style of the work selected
- a review of a performance
- an account from the point of view of a minor character in the selected work

Is the creative option for you?

The creative assignment is a very popular option, and may look easier or more fun than the others, but in fact often requires more skill and certainly as much discipline as the other possibilities. It is very often poorly done, needlessly bringing candidates' grades down, so you need to be careful, as well as honest about your own capacities, before choosing this option.

For example, if you are a talented Theatre Arts or Drama student, with experience in directing, the letter to an actor about his or her part in a play could be an excellent way of using your particular skills. Similarly, if you are a good writer sensitive to style, writing in the style of an author (creating a 'pastiche') can be a challenging and worthwhile exercise. You could also write from the point of view of a character whose thoughts are not represented in any detail in your text (for example, Greta the sister in *Metamorphosis*).

You need to remember that whatever you do, the result will be judged by the same criteria as World Literature One. You must ask yourself the question: *How does my idea allow me to show good knowledge of and good insight into the text?* However clever and original your idea may be, if it does not do this, you cannot do well on the paper.

A 'diary' of a character that is merely a paraphrase of some parts of the text, with no sensitivity to the style such a character would write in has little if any merit. Similarly, if you have little or no experience of theatre or film, you should not be attempting to play director to an actor. An example of a creative assignment is given below which illustrates how creativity and understanding of the text may successfully be combined.

The Importance of the 'statement of intent' in the creative option

All creative assignments must be preceded by a 'statement of intent', without which your work cannot be appropriately evaluated. You should carefully consult the regulations for guidance on this. It should identify the text inspiring the project, the kind of task to be undertaken, the aspects of the text on which the task will be based, and how you intend to explore these aspects (the sample below illustrates these clearly). Your grasp of the text and its style, as well as your purpose in undertaking this, should be clear from this 'statement of intent' which is included in your word count.

If you know that your experience and skills have not prepared you for this kind of assignment, look at the other options.

Sample of the Imaginative or Creative Assignment

As you read through the following statement of intent of a creative piece on Allende's *House of the Spirits*, note in what ways it reflects knowledge and understanding of the text.

"No Brushstroke is in vain": a continuation of the Trueba saga through the years of military dictatorship under General Augusto Pinochet Ugarte

Statement of Intent.

The following passages are episodes of Alba Trueba's life, beginning from the end of Isabel Allende's novel the <u>House of the Spirits</u>*, following her as she gives birth to her daughter, and endures life in a repressed Chile, awaiting the day when her lover Miguel can return and begin life with his family in a restored democracy. I have tried to capture Allende's use of magical realism, jumbled chronology, narrative voices, and hyperbole of characterization to bring alive the family's vibrant eccentricities, and fold the nation's history into their story.*

Aura's name, just like generations of Del Valle women, carries connotations of light, clarity and pallid beauty. Aura, meaning sunrise, is also translated as aura, which continues the maternal lineage associated with spirituality and psychic intuition. Aura is the heart of the family's continued history, embodying both the heritage of Alba's family —with the reappearance of beauty, mystic qualities, flight, and invented beasts — as well as her father's traits, with her sad eyes, revolutionary spirit, and reluctance to cry.

Aura is haunted by the dark and unsettling presence of Esteban Garcia who is a constant reminder of her mother Alba's past and her struggle to become reconciled with it. His presence is manifested in the shadow that lingers in Aura's eyes, and the bouts of physical pain she endures, re-living her mother's torture, and inflicting her childhood with consequences of the past. The spirit of Clara cares for Aura during those attacks, her strength and healing presence becoming a symbol of the human spirit that survives throughout the novel, waiting with other spirits of the house to be free from military dictatorship.

The big house on the corner continues to be used as a microcosm of Chile, evolving as Chile did during the years of military dictatorship under Pinoche. As Chile is renovated to hide poverty and the destruction of the 1973 coup d'etat, the big house is given the same illusionary beauty and economic prosperity, but underneath the gilded layer of militaristic order, the reality is much different. At the end of the passages, the true condition of the house is seen, and the spirits are once again free to inhabit the chipped walls and scratched marble floors.

The passages are divided into three groups, replicating the different narrators in the novel, beginning with Alba as she continues the narrative from the end of the novel. The second group of passages are written in the anonymous third-person narrative that is used for much of the novel as Alba re-writes Clara's chronicles of the past "according to events and not to chronological order". The final section is told by Miguel as he travels home from exile, a parallel to Esteban Trueba's narrative as he works to amass his fortune in the mines, and his descriptions of his journeys home to see his family.

Through research (see the bibliography) and careful analysis of the text, I have tried to capture the essence of Allende's writing and to use similar tone and descriptive techniques to bring alive the magic realism of her work and balance it with the reality of the family's life and the cyclical nature of their history.

You will see that the candidate has grasped fully the significance, main features, content and style of the novel before embarking on the piece. You would have little sense of the depth and relevance of the extra chapter without this insight into his knowledge and response. This illustrates the way in which discipline and tautness of approach complements, and is indispensable to, the creative aspect. The statement of intent is as important as the creative writing: he makes clear what he is going to do and why, and then does it. In addition, as he shows in his bibliography (not illustrated here), the candidate has brought the novel up-to-date through his own reading in Chile's more recent history – a good example of appropriate use of secondary sources. The extra section follows here, linked to the work by the quotation from the end of *House of the Spirits*.

"I want to think that my task is life and my mission is not to prolong hatred but simply fill these pages while I wait for Miguel, while I bury my grandfather, whose body lies beside me in this room, while I wait for better times to come..."

Better times did come. It was more than sixteen years after our trip into the mountains and our final goodbye that I saw Miguel again. My grandfather left me in the big house on the corner, knowing that one day I would retrieve the love I once knew, but with a wisdom from my past and the words left by Clara. The freshness of the winter quickly faded as if time had melted overnight. I could smell the sultry heat of the summer months approaching, but the bitterness of the stinging cold still lingered throughout the house, one that would remain for many years to come. The outside had been restored to its former beauty, the stained glass windows glistened and the Italian marble floors reflected like mirrors at the Palace of Versailles.

At the height of my reconciliation with the past, beautiful Aura was born. The ease and tranquillity with which she arrived differed from the pain that plagued her conception. I gave birth alone, on my grandmother's sailboat, a light breeze stirring the white veil above the bed. The room was filled with hidden spirits, among them Clara, who once more came to be my pillar of strength. I sat with our daughter in my warms as the sun rose above the horizon and shone through the open window, wrapping around Aura like a swarm of bees. She was a perfect creature, with Rosa's beauty, Clara's strength, and her father's sad eyes. She never cried throughout her infancy, going from silence to her very first words. She didn't need years; her eyes were enough. They had the power to communicate every thought, every feeling that she was experiencing. The deep blue centres covered in a grey, looming shadow that made even her laughter seem unusually distressing.

I received my first letter from Miguel the day Aura was born. He told me not to try to reply or discover where the letters were coming from, and our relationship continued on the memories of the love and passion we once shared. He didn't know that I had been pregnant and he wouldn't know of his daughter's existence until much later, when those who fled could return home.

****

On the night of Aura's third birthday her attacks began. Alba awoke suffocating as though she was being strangled and ran to see Aura, sensing that something was wrong with the child. Aura was silently shaking in her bed, sweat dripping down her forehead with her neck pulled tightly against her shoulders. Alba looked into her eyes and screamed at the pain her child was re-living. Clara held the child in her arms and calmed her body. The attacks continued, interrupting Aura's childhood with her family's past and injecting her life with a poison that Alba was determined to break.

As Aura learned to read, she would spend more and more time in her great-grandfather's library. She developed a love for literature and poetry and became fascinated with the Poet and his epic poems, which made her blood boil with a familiar revolutionary passion. Aura found what was left of Uncle Marco's treasures, as well as boxes of her great-uncle Jaime's books, and the old dining room table that Nicolas once taught his eager female admiradoras on. When she was seven years old, Aura found a book on the history of flight, and became fascinated with the Eastern traditions of kite-making. That evening at dinner, Aura announced that she was going to conquer gravity just as her uncles before her had tried to do. Alba laughed quietly to herself knowing that it was inevitable. With guidance from her book, and inspiration deep within her, Aura created soaring beasts that graced the sky with their terrible presence. Great phoenixes in pyres of brilliant purple and red, alongside gigantic horned monsters, were urged higher into the clouds with silent encouragement from Uncle Marcos and Nicolas.

****

It was the happiest day of my life when I heard from Alba for the first time in almost twenty years. The dictatorship had finally ended, and it was time to build the future Alba and I had waited so long for. That was the day I learned about my daughter, Aura the Beautiful. The day of that victorious election, I made arrangements to return home. I spoke with Alba for only a few short minutes, her voice stronger than I had ever heard it and freer than it had ever been. At last I had my family, the woman I loved, and the child I never knew but would love for an eternity.

I arrived on the street where the big house stood with the clouds moving in the aftermath of a storm. I looked down the long lane of mansions, the musty smell of my surroundings reminding me of the illusion they had lived in. I walked towards the house, every step bringing me closer to the beginning of my life. As I arrived at the house, the restored façade that had been preserved through those long years suddenly lost its lustre, but inside, a light filled the house. The spirits were finally free, no longer hidden by the perfectly aligned carpets and polished crystal chandeliers.

The clouds opened up above the house and a ray of light illuminated a distant creature bobbing gently in the breeze. It was a magical beast, burning in the heavenly glow as if its soul was being born, its neck outstretched to take its first breath of life. I followed the glow down towards the front steps of the big house. There, an angel stood to greet me, the light crowning her like a coronet of orange roses. I looked up at her face and watched as a fog lifted from her eyes to reveal a beauty that had been plagued for so many years. This was Aura, my Aura. Better times had come.

3. Detailed Study

There are four possibilities in this section:

a) A 'formal' essay

This is the kind of essay in which you have probably had the most experience: the essay on a single topic, based on a single work. It is an opportunity to explore a specific aspect of one World Literature text in a straightforward way, with an argument clearly running through the essay. For example: "The implications of weather in *One Day in the Life of Ivan Denisovitch*", or "The role of the Gods in *Antigone*". As with World Literature One, it is an opportunity to explore an aspect that echoes your own interests. For example, one candidate who had a strong interest in music, wrote very perceptively on the use and effect of different instruments in Chekhov's *Three Sisters*.

b) Analysis of a key passage

The focus of this should be showing *why it is 'key' to our understanding of the text it comes from*, though the passage may also be explored from a number of different angles: style, character, plot, theme, language, etc. The treatment of the passage should look outwards to relate it to the rest of the text You will probably have had quite a bit of practice in analysing and discussing key passages in the course of studying many of your texts (for example in preparing for your formal oral) so this too should be a familiar and fairly 'safe' choice, though to do it well requires skill. A key passage from Marquez's *Chronicle of a Death Foretold* could be the brutal and extraordinary description of the 'foretold' killing of Santiago Nasar towards the end of the novel.

c) Analysis of two key passages

The passages should form an interesting comparison and contrast within the same text and, as in the previous option, should be shown as pivotal to the work they come from. For example, Antigone's outrage at her imagined spectacle of her brother's unburied body, at the beginning of the play, might be paired and contrasted with Tiresius's outraged, imagined description of the ravaged body towards the end of the play. An early dialogue between Nora and Torvald in *A Doll's House* could be compared with the conversation they have before Nora leaves.

You may also compare a key passage from a World Literature work with a passage from another work (not a World Literature work) in the programme. This too can lead to a very individual and imaginative choice.

d) Commentary on an extract from a work

You need to distinguish this from the *key passage* above. The focus of the commentary is on *the detailed analysis of the passage itself*, though it may imply or refer to the wider relevance of the extract. Unlike the key passage, you are restricted to about 30 lines. It is an opportunity to choose an extract to which you have had a particular, personal response, and to show (as one might in the written commentary on the exam) awareness of how imagery, style, themes, character, etc. work in the passage. You cannot, however, use this option to translate a passage from the original text and comment on the translation.

From the following example you can see that such a commentary allows you considerable scope to display your particular interests and expertise, within a framework you should be familiar and comfortable with from your work on the exam commentary and the formal oral commentary. It also provides good practice for the formal oral commentary and the exam commentary

Sample of Detailed Study: commentary on an extract (from the opening of the essay)

Close commentary on <u>Hedda Gabler</u>, *Act Two (Pages 319 –321): an examination of the importance of this passage in understanding Hedda's psychology and her relationship with those around her.*

In this passage of "Hedda Gabler" by Ibsen, we are faced with a crucial moment in the play. It presents the beginning of the downfall of Eilert Lovberg as Hedda systematically goes about destroying that which she loves but cannot (or will not) have. Hedda's need to dominate and control, shown so strikingly here, seems to stem from her unhappiness with her own situation. It gives her an illusion of control over her life, and will be taken to an extreme within this scene. In a sense, this is the climax of the play, as what follows later shows the inevitable consequences of the action here. We also see the superficial and oppressive qualities of the bourgeois society of Norway then, which will rule and ruin the lives of those involved.

The passage is from the end of Act Two, and deals with Hedda, Eilert Lovborg and Thea Elvsted. It begins with Hedda directing Thea, Lovborg's new companion, and Lovborg, to sit on either side of her. "I want to be in the middle". The fact that she is giving orders (which is characteristic of her) foretells her actions to come, which will dictate the future of Lovberg and consequently Thea. As importantly, her placing of herself separating them symbolizes the wedge she is soon to drive between them. Her situating herself "in the middle" is key to our understanding her relationship with all around her. Throughout the play we see her placing herself between Tesman her husband, and their mutual friend Brack ; between Tesman and his aunt Miss Tesman, between Miss Tesman and Berte the maid.

Ibsen has carefully prepared us for this moment and the struggle for Lovborg, through Hedda's conversation with Thea in Act One where she prods Thea in order to understand the nature of her relationship with Lovborg; and through her daringly intimate conversation with Lovborg shortly before this, from which she might deduce that she still has influence over him, and which arms her for the fight. Ibsen has also prepared the ground carefully in terms of placing Lovborg within a wider context of struggle – the professional competition with Tesman and the sexual and territorial competition with Brack for Hedda. Physically this competition is emphasised here by the two groups: Tesman and Brack in the inner room. Lovborg, Thea and Hedda centre stage. Socially, Lovborg 'belongs' with the men (and will indeed leave with them later); emotionally, he belongs with the women, both of whom offer him something different, important, and mutually exclusive. Within the outwardly decorous setting of the Tesmans' formal drawing room where all these characters are met, and the formality of manners and conversation, deadly conflicts are now developed.

*Lovborg begins the conversation. Through his comments about Thea he is making a comparison between her and Hedda. This is important as it sets up the parallel in his relationship with each. He then contrast the two of them by his statement that "We two –she and I -, we really are comrades". The pronouns "we", "she", "I" and the present tense "are", all draw attention to Hedda as of the past, and Thea of the present, especially as "comrades" was Hedda's definition of her relationship with Lovborg. Possibly Lovborg is aiming to hurt Hedda with his statements; surely he is presenting the fact that Thea was able to go through with her desires. At this point Hedda gives away a great deal about herself, when Lovborg mentions admiringly that Thea has courage. Hedda says, as if to herself, "Ah, courage. Yes. If one only had that… then perhaps one could even **live** at last". We have had the sense all along that Hedda is not living, but just drifting through her existence. Her lack of courage to follow her desires, and thus live, must be unbearable, especially faced with one who does. It is at this moment that, with a change of tone, she begins her attack on Lovborg with her offer of a drink, as if in retaliation for her unhappiness.*

Comment on the sample

This candidate has chosen a rewarding passage for commentary, and explores it from a number of angles, especially character, carefully reading the subtext of the dialogue and the language used for clues to action. He also shows good awareness of the significance of staging and stage directions.

Checklist for World Literature Assignment Two

First, look again at the checklist for Assignment One, as many of the same questions apply, especially 1, 2, 3, 5, 6, and 8

1. Have you clearly indicated the nature of the assignment. For example: Assignment 2(a): Comparative Study?

2. If you have written a creative assignment, does your statement of intent cover all the requirements for this? Look back at the sample above. Does your assignment meet the assessment criteria?

3. If you have written a commentary on an extract, have you included copies of the passage(s), attached to your assignment?

4. Have you included a bibliography? The edition and translation of your text(s) should be included, together with any other sources used, including internet sources.

5. Are you within the word count – no more than 10% above or below the limit? Have you given an accurate total?

6. Where relevant, have you provided a carefully selected title that clearly indicates the topic?

Glossary

This glossary contains many of the commonly used terms in literary analysis and appreciation that may come your way in the A1 programme. Don't learn them off by heart, but try to become familiar with as many as you can so as to have greater control and understanding in your reading and writing. The most important thing is to see how the terms function, and to become alert to these effects in your reading. As far as possible, illustrations are drawn from this Guide. How many of these do you already know? How many would you feel comfortable applying in your work? Chapters One, Two, and Three, contain further discussion of terms.

Alienation: This term, from Marxism, suggests that under Capitalism we live estranged from our true human natures.

✓**Allegory:** A story of some complexity that corresponds to another situation on a deeper level. *Animal Farm* is about a community of animals, but reflects the Russian Revolution and satirises Communism. The dual perspective, the link between animal story and political story gives it its interest and wit.

✓**Alliteration:** Repetition of an identical consonant sound at the beginning of stressed words, usually close together ("*So dawn goes down to day*" : Frost) Look at the effect alliteration creates. It may for example draw together *unlike* ideas for contrast, or suggest meaning through the sound effect (as in the Frost line, suggesting depressing inevitability), or link *similar* things for emphasis. Used in both poetry and prose.

✓**Allusion:** A reference to an event, person, place, work of literature etc. that gives additional layers of meaning to a text or enlarges its frame of reference. Look at the biblical allusion to the "whited sepulchre" in the Conrad essay sample, Chapter Two of this Guide.

Ambiguity: (Distinguish this from ambivalence). Where language and tone are (usually deliberately), unclear and may have two or more interpretations or meanings. Look at the discussion of Banquo's speech in Chapter Four of this Guide.

Ambivalence: Where the writer's attitude to, for example, a character or event is not clear-cut, but may seem to hold at least two responses (Marlow's attitude to Kurtz in Conrad's *Heart of Darkness* - both understanding *and* critical?).

Antithesis: Contrasting ideas by balancing words of opposite meaning and idea ("And wretches *hang*, that jurymen may *dine*": Alexander Pope).

✓**Apostrophe:** An exclamatory passage where the speaker or writer breaks off in the flow of a narrative or poem to address a dead or absent person, a particular audience, or object (often personified). Gaev in Chekhov's *Cherry Orchard* addresses a bookcase at length, symbol of his past and the family home.

✓**Assonance:** Repetition of similar vowel sounds close to one another ("Down some profound dull tunnel" Wilfred Owen). Can create atmosphere in descriptive poetry. Sound this aloud to hear the effect.

Atmosphere: Often confused with 'mood', it refers specifically to *place*, a setting, or surroundings. ("There was a holiday atmosphere in the town".)

Bathos: A sudden descent from the sublime or serious, to the ridiculous or trivial. "His pride and his bicycle tyre were punctured in the first hour".

Bildungsroman: German term for a novel focusing on the development of a character from youth to maturity. (Joyce: *Portrait of the Artist as a Young Man* is a famous example of a male; *Jane Eyre* of a female.)

✓**Blank verse:** Unrhymed poetry not broken into stanzas, keeping to a strict pattern in each line, usually in iambic pentameter. Used by Shakespeare, epic poets, and much of Frost. It is close to the rhythm of speech. (Chapter Four: Orals – "Upon my head they placed a fruitless crown".) Sound it out to find the pattern of those five stressed syllables, but observe how close to speech rhythms it is.

✓**Caesura:** A break or pause *within a line* of poetry by comma or full stop or unmarked pause, used for emphasis, or to change direction or pace. Quite frequently used, so worth knowing. (Look at the "Black Lace Fan" in the Commentary Chapter: "He was always late. That evening he was later".)

Caricature: An exaggerated representation of a character often by emphasising a small number of features, usually for comic and satiric purposes. Jane Austen and Dickens frequently use this.

Colloquial: Everyday speech and language as opposed to literary or formal register. The inclusion of the odd colloquial word or phrase in an otherwise formal work can be striking. Look at *The Horse's Mouth*, in the Commentary Chapter where literary and colloquial registers mix.

Conceit: A witty thought or idea or image, a fanciful or deliberately far-fetched comparison, as found in 16th and 17th century English poetry. Donne compares two lovers to the points of a mathematical compass.

Concrete: (As in concrete detail). Refers to objects or aspects that may be perceived by the senses.

Connotation: An association that a word may suggest. Very useful word when discussing diction.

Consonance: Where the final consonants are the same in two or more words close together, as in Macbeth's "poor player/That *struts and frets* his hour upon the stage".

Contradiction: (Distinguish from 'paradox'). Stating or implying the opposite of what has been said or suggested.

Couplet (rhyming couplet): Two consecutive rhyming lines of verse. May clinch or emphasise an idea (*Nature's first green is gold/ Her hardest hue to hold*' : Frost)

Defamiliarization: The technique of making the familiar seem new and strange, and thus making us see more vividly. Coined by the Russian "Formalists". This may be done through point of view, as in *Gulliver's Travels*.

Denouement: Literally, from the French, 'unknotting'. How the ending of a novel or play turns out, how the plot is unravelled or revealed.

Diction: The writer's choice of words or vocabulary. You will need this word.

Didactic: Describes the tone or intention to preach a (usually) moral, political or religious point. It usually has a negative connotation.

Dramatic irony: A very powerful tool especially in drama, used for tragic or comic purposes. Where a character (or characters) is/are unaware of something that the audience/reader and possibly other characters on stage are aware of.

Elegy: A mournful lament for times past or the dead. It has a particular poetic form but the term can be used more generally. "Elegiac" describes a meditative mood in prose or verse, reflecting on the past.

End-stopped line: A line of poetry where the meaning pauses or stops at the end of the line ("Nature's first green is gold": Frost) A statement or idea can stand out clearly, and provide a pause for reflection.

Enjambement: The opposite of the above. The sense flows over from one line to another, perhaps even to the next stanza. This can reflect a build-up of emotion or create dramatic effect (see the final stanza of "Dulce Et Decorum Est", Chapter Four: Orals). From the French for "leg".

Epigram: A concise, pointed, witty statement. 'Epigrammatic' style in prose or poetry has those qualities. Oscar Wilde is a master of epigram:" The truth is rarely pure and never simple".

Form: A word that often crops up and seems vague, but is important. It is the shape of a work, the arrangement of its parts, the patterns, divisions and structures used. In poetry there are traditional, metrical and rhyming 'forms' (ode, ballad, sonnet, etc.), and modern, non-metrical forms. If you want to know what these are, consult further resources for this.

Free verse: Verse written without any fixed or traditional structure in metre or rhyme. Commonly used since the early 20th century. It is very flexible because it follows the speech rhythms of the language.

Genre: A specific type or kind of literature, such as drama, prose, poetry, essay, autobiography.

Grain: ('Reading against the grain'). A reader can go acceptingly along with assumptions and values in a text, or go 'against the grain', resisting and questioning values and assumptions in that text, as Feminist critics often advocate when reading books by male authors. It can also apply to a number of other situations including, for example, the reading of books written in the colonial period.

Hyperbole: A deliberate exaggeration for various effects, comic, tragic, etc. When Frost writes that the beauty of Spring "is only so an hour", he emphasises the tragic brevity of life.

Iambic: This you *must* know. The 'iamb' is a metrical measure, or foot, in which an unstressed syllable is followed by a stressed syllable ("He clasps"). Iambic pentameter (five iambs in a line) is the commonest metrical pattern in English poetry, including Shakespeare.("Upon my head they placed a fruitless crown": Macbeth. Sound it out to find those five stresses.) Note that you can have other kinds of iambic line such as the four-iamb line, called tetrameter (see "The Eagle" in Chapter One).

Idyll/idyllic: Refers to innocent simple life in idealised rural setting. An "idyllic" childhood or country scene or experience has those untroubled, and simple qualities. Useful adjective.

Imagery: Used frequently –another word you need. It means concrete descriptions (images) we can see and sense in works of literature. Wilfred Owen (Chapter Four: Orals) describes a dying soldier with "white eyes writhing in his face". We see (whites of eyes rolling, his face) and feel ("writhing") the agony.

Interior monologue: See Chapter Two, novel section, for definition

Internal rhyme: Where there are rhymes within a line instead of, or as well as, at the ends of lines.

Irony: A difficult term to define, often used wrongly, and an effect that is often missed when analysing literature. It means a gap or mismatch between what is being said, and what is intended, perhaps between the way a character or group sees him/her/itself, and the way the author wishes us to see him/her/it. (See the analysis of the opening of *Pride and Prejudice* in Chapter Two of this Guide). A powerful tool for a writer as it exposes hypocrisies and lack of awareness. (Distinguish from dramatic irony.)

Lyric: Originally a song performed to a lyre (early harp); now, a songlike poem expressing personal feeling. A common form. Prose can be lyrical too, expressive of feelings.

Metaphor: You can't get far without this. A comparison of two things without using a comparing word such as "like". To see a striking similarity between two normally unlike things can be an indicator of originality. It provides richness of sensation and meaning. The comparison may be implied rather than spelt out. Wilfred Owen's description of the dying soldier "guttering" is comparing him implicitly with a candle flame on the point of going out.

Metre: The organization of lines of verse into regular patterns of stressed and unstressed syllables to achieve a rhythmic effect. Seems frightening and complicated, but a good resource book or teacher can make it clear. Helpful to understand the essentials, but not mandatory.

Mimesis: A term not so commonly used, but it describes an interesting and common effect: the use of words that suggest movement, shape, size, texture (smooth, rough, soft). Wilfred Owen's description of the gas attack: " An ecstasy of fumbling/ Fitting the clumsy helmets just in time" has a *mimetic* effect, suggesting panic and confusion of movement.

Mood: (Often confused with atmosphere and tone) Refers to people as in "the mood of the audience was sombre". Describes a person's (a character's or the narrator's) frame of mind or state of feeling. It may also indicate the emotional response the author hopes to evoke in the mind of the reader.

Monologue: Speech, usually of some length, by a single speaker. Distinguish from soliloquy. A 'dramatic' monologue' (usually a whole poem) has a listener present and reveals the character of the speaker in a striking way. (Some of Browning's and Frost's poems)

Motif: Often used synonymously with the German *leitmotif*, meaning recurrent elements (images, ideas) in a work. These are not as significant as themes but have a cumulative effect like a refrain, and can assume symbolic importance. Candles and fire in *Great Expectations* could be seen in this way.

Omniscient Narrator: It literally means 'all-knowing", describing one who stands outside and can see into all characters and happenings, like Jane Austen.

Onomatopoeia: The effect of words that imitate the sound of things ("hiss", "crash").

Oxymoron: Where two words of opposite meaning are joined – "An open secret". It can suggest something quite complex or provocative.

Paradox: (Distinguish this from contradiction and oxymoron). Seemingly contradictory statement, but on reflection, it makes sense, contains its own resolution or truth ('Nature's first green is gold': Robert Frost. Green can't be gold literally, but the earliest signs of life in spring may be precious, like gold).

Parody: Usually comic imitation of another work. Distinguish from *pastiche* (an option in World Literature 2)

Pastiche: A literary work composed in the style of a well-known author.

Persona: The identity or character assumed by the author in a work of literature

Personification: Where human feelings or sensations are attributed to an inanimate object. Human qualities may also be given to abstract ideas.

Plot: (Distinguish from story, which lists the events of a narrative in chronological order). Plot refers to the events of a narrative in the order the author has *chosen* to present them. Chronology may be distorted for particular effects, as in flashbacks or flash forwards. A novel may begin with the ending of the story, for example.

Point of view: A key concept in literature especially the novel, but can be confusing. It is The angle from which the narrative is seen or told. Who sees? Who speaks? The point of view may shift in a work (see Chapter Two and Three for more).

Protagonist: Main character in a work

Quatrain: Stanza or group of four lines that can have different rhyme schemes. Shakespeare's sonnets often contain three quatrains and a couplet.

Refrain: Repetition in a work of literature of a phrase or lines.

Rhythm: Distinguish this from metre, which has to do with the *technical, identifiable* organization of lines into units of stressed and unstressed syllables. Rhythm applies to both prose and poetry and has to do more generally with the flow of sound created by stressed and unstressed syllables.(Steady, irregular?)

Satire: Exposing and ridiculing of human follies in a society, sometimes with the aim to reform, sometimes predominantly to deflate. May be gentle, comic, biting or bitter, or a combination. Chaucer, Swift, Jane Austen and Dickens use this tool memorably.

Setting: Context in which a work of literature takes place: geographical, social, historical, generalized, conventional, symbolic, etc. See Chapter Two for more details.

Simile: Where a comparison is made explicit with 'as' or 'like' (distinguish from metaphor). Can make descriptions vivid and unusual. Dickens is a master of the simile.

Skaz: (From the Russian). A technique of narration that mirrors oral narration with its hesitations, corrections, grammatical mistakes, interactions, etc. *Catcher in the Rye* uses this, but also *Huckleberry Finn*, amongst others.

Soliloquy: A speech by a character alone on stage, thinking aloud, revealing thoughts and emotions, or communicating directly with the audience. Powerful tool for revealing psychological complexity, used often by Shakespeare.

Sonnet: A fourteen-line rhyming poem often in iambic pentameter. Rhyme schemes and organization of lines vary, depending on the type of sonnet (for example, Shakespearian), but often set out as a block of 8 lines (octave) and six lines (sestet).

Stanza: The blocks of lines into which a poem is organized. In traditional forms of poetry each stanza follows a scheme governing metre, lines and rhymes.

Story: (Distinguish this from plot). The events of a narrative in the chronological order in which they actually happened.

Stream of consciousness: (See Chapter Two) The impression of a random stream of thoughts.

Style: Necessary concept to know and use, but tricky to define and discuss. It has to do with the distinctive traits in an author's work, the 'how' of writing. It concerns theme, diction (emotional, abstract, poetic), sentence construction, imagery, sound, etc.

Subtext: Ideas, feelings, thoughts, not dealt with directly in the text but existing underneath. Quite a useful concept especially when reading plays, as characters don't always express their real thoughts.

Symbol: Objects that represent or evoke an idea or concept of wider, abstract significance, as roses represent love, walls divisions.

Syntax: (See the discussion in Chapter One of this Guide) The grammatical structure of words in a sentence. The normal order of words can be slightly displaced to create a particular effect, without losing the sense. Macbeth: "Upon my head they placed a fruitless crown".

Theme: Central ideas or issues, often abstract (for example racial injustice) explored or illustrated in a text. Can also refer to an argument raised or pursued in a text, like a thesis.

Tone: (Distinguish from mood, above.) The *technique* of writing to convey the attitude of the writer towards his/her subject. Created through aspects of language like diction, syntax, rhythm, which will suggest a 'tone of voice'. Emotional meaning. See discussion on Wilfred Owen in Chapter One.

Trochee/ trochaic: The reverse of iambic, as in: "Mary had a little lamb". It may be used as a contrast within an iambic line, to stress an idea (as at the beginning of lines two and three of "The Eagle", Chapter One, where it emphasises the visual image).